Praise for *The St*

"A complex tale about deception and revelation as profoundly confessional as *The Liars' Club,* and a great job of storytelling—in *The Strongbox,* reluctant sleuth Terry Sue Harms sifts through clues to a dark past in a relentless probe for identity."

—Linda Watanabe McFerrin,
author of *Dead Love* and *Navigating the Divide*

"The most compelling thing I've read in years. The elements of this true story are fascinating in and of themselves: addiction, grinding poverty, abusive parenting, glamour, recovery, true romance, spirit rising strong and beautiful. But even more engaging than the subject itself is the gripping and lyrical way Harms writes. This is not only the author's story but also a light on the path for many, many others."

—Kathryn Page, PhD,
president of FASD NorCal

"*The Strongbox* is not just a spectacular story, it's also a cathartic one. Rejection, shame, and insecurity are universal shadows we all have, and Terry, with her rough start in life, plucky curiosity, and intelligent drive, is beautifully aware of her shadows—enough to look them in the face and give them a voice but not let them run the show."

—Nicole Fuller, MAT,
holistic health coach

THE
STRONGBOX

SEARCHING FOR
MY ABSENT FATHER

TERRY SUE HARMS

She Writes Press, a BookSparks imprint
A Division of SparkPointStudio, LLC.

Published 2020
Printed in the United States of America

Print ISBN: 978-1-63152-775-3
E-ISBN: 978-1-63152-776-0
Library of Congress Control Number: 2020909025

For information, address:
She Writes Press
1569 Solano Ave #546
Berkeley, CA 94707

She Writes Press is a division of SparkPoint Studio, LLC.

This memoir is dedicated

to

those who struggle with

reading.

I know how it feels.

AUTHOR'S NOTE

Many of the names in this memoir have been changed. Where actual names have been used, it was done with explicit permission or when the named person is no longer living. Where names have been changed, those changes were done for my benefit alone. Because this story is about me, I felt it was unnecessary to expose any individuals by their true names.

Beyond that, I've made every attempt to be truthful and have not embellished any details to make for a more entertaining read; I didn't have to.

God knows, I'm humbled and grateful to have gotten here from there.

He who learns must suffer.
And even in our sleep,
pain that cannot forget
falls drop by drop upon the heart,
and in our own despair,
against our will,
comes wisdom to us by the awful grace of God.

Aeschylus
Ancient Greece

Ellis vs. Abbott." That indented heading sits at the top of two letters written between attorneys that have been in my possession for over four decades. One is dated January 18, 1967, and the other was written two months later, on March 27. The documents are copies of the originals. Xerographic printing in the early 1960s was something to be proud of, and "Xero Copy" is conspicuously inked across the top border of each document. The faded letters emit a scent reminiscent of old shoes and musty linens, and I always feel the need to wash my hands after touching them. Both were written by a lawyer named Gene Rhodes, and their recipient was "Attorney at Law," Mr. Charles R. Way.

The first letter reads:

Dear Mr. Way:

Enclosed are copies of our correspondence over the past several months. In your September 26th letter, you stated that you would be discussing the child support matter with your client, and would let us know accordingly.

Since that time, we wrote you another letter on October 20, 1966 stating our client's wishes. However, as of that date we have had no reply from you.

Would you please contact us at your earliest convenience with regards to the proposal as outlined in the October 20th letter.

Thank you for your cooperation herein.

Very truly yours, Gene Rhodes

And the second:

Pursuant to our discussions with your office this date, our client is acceptable to Mr. Abbott's offer of $20.00 per week for child support. Would you please make arrangements with him to effect the increase as soon as possible.

Thank you for your courtesy in this matter.

The two letters were copied to Mrs. Margaret G, my mother, who died suddenly and unexpectedly when I was sixteen. I would have been six years old when my mother's attorney wrote those letters; my brother Sean would have been nine. When my mother died, it was my understanding that Mr. Abbott—a man I'd never met and my mother almost never talked about—was Sean's and my father.

My mother kept those letters in a dented metal file box she called "the strongbox." For many years, the name itself—the strongbox—was symbolic of what that box came to mean to me. That steel repository was my mother's system of record, and like a Delphic oracle, it contained hidden messages and a mystical force that I sought and feared in equal measure. I believed the strongbox would someday unravel my tangled, mostly missing family history and lead me to all the answers I was seeking in life. Not only was I eager to discover the truth about my father—who he was and why he was never part of the family—but I also wanted to understand the disaster zone my childhood became in his absence. My mother was an alcoholic and died young. My stepfather, LG, was emotionally abusive and mentally unstable. My siblings and I had almost nothing to do with one another. Furthermore, we were desperately poor. There was always money for cigarettes, beer, and gallons of vodka, but breakfast might be dry cereal; lunch could be mustard and mayonnaise sandwiches; and dinner, canned hash.

Of course, I had no way of knowing what role my father's absence played in this toxic family drama. For all I knew, my mother kicked him out (or never invited him in) because he was even more of a nightmare than my stepfather. Feeling lonely, insecure, and afraid (but determined not to succumb to the madness around me), I convinced myself that the missing father of my dreams—Mr. Abbott in the strongbox, perhaps—was the key to making my life better.

This book is about my forty-year quest to find that man and see if I was right.

On February 12, 1977—the year before I ran away from home—my mother and my stepfather, LG, went out to celebrate Valentine's Day and LG's forty-third birthday. The two hadn't had a titanic clash in a couple of years, but as the night wore on with no sign of their return, memories of their knock-down, drag-out fights, always fueled by alcohol, began to swell in me.

They said they were going out to dinner, so I expected them home by nine o'clock at the latest. When they weren't home by ten, I instinctively understood that dinner had turned into dinner and drinks. LG was a bartender at a dive joint in an area crawling with pimps, prostitutes, drug addicts, and white-collar professionals attempting to hide their addictions. LG and my mother, with keys to the bar and nobody to tell them otherwise, would be able to drink as much, and as long, as they wanted.

I had reason to worry. Their last big scene, two years earlier, had gotten so violent that the police had taken Sean and me away to a child-welfare shelter. I had been the one to call for help. I remember dialing 0 on a rotary phone. In a whisper, I explained to the operator that my parents were fighting and that I was afraid. When the police arrived, I was desperate that they not tell on me for pulling such a stunt. I knew not to interfere with my parents' business. I hadn't been spanked since I was a small child, but more than once I had heard, "Quit crying or I will give you something to cry about," which I always took to mean some sort of physical punishment: slapping, pinching, or pulling my hair (the latter having the advantage of not leaving a mark). Even if there was no actual beating, I knew the agony of my mother's scornful silence, and I cowered at the thought of it being turned on me.

When I called for the police, I hadn't guessed that Sean and I would be the ones to get hauled off. I assumed they'd take LG. I didn't want to go, but at the same time I was relieved to get away from the hitting and screaming.

Once we arrived at the child-welfare facility, Sean was sent to the boy's wing, and I was ushered down a corridor to sleep with the girls. The next morning I was shown to an industrial-style bathroom: a bank of sinks and toilet stalls, and showers with no privacy curtains. There were older girls milling around, some naked and far more developed than I was, their breasts and pubic hair a declaration of their superiority. One girl was skillfully applying thick black eyeliner. I turned away when she gave me a warning look.

By day's end, my internment was over. No charges had been filed against LG, and he came by himself to pick up Sean and me. The drive home was silent. Once we arrived, I saw my mother; her face was swollen and bruised almost beyond recognition. He had done that to her. Nobody talked about it, and the next morning I went to school pretending that nothing of note had occurred over the weekend.

The Valentine's Day date night was preceded by those two years of calm. But within a mere few hours, I was pulled back into the ugly past in a kind of PTSD loop: the hollering, the brutal attacks, the hitting until someone passed out or the police arrived.

There were times when I had pleaded with my mother to leave LG, assuring her that we would be better off without him. She wouldn't hear it. Her justification for staying was always the old adage "It's better to live with the devil you know than the one you don't." I couldn't understand that.

She never would have stood for me continuing to play with a friend who stole my toys. If I had said it was okay because I always *knew* my friend was a thief, she would have scolded me for my idiocy and sent me to my room. Obviously, though, I didn't have the same authority to challenge *her* excuses.

So as "last call" approached on that tension-filled night, when the bars are supposed to close, my cochlear nerves and every receptive fiber in my ears were at full attention. I listened for the car to round the corner. I listened for Mom and LG to shuffle down the sidewalk in case they had decided to take the bus home. I was in bed, but every few minutes I lifted my head off the pillow to squint at the clock, and as time went on, I got more and more nervous, assuming that the more hours that went by, the more drinks the two would be downing.

When the sun came up the next morning and they still weren't home, I ached with dread. They had never pulled an all-nighter before. I tried to bury my anxiety, hoping that with the light of day, they would get breakfast somewhere and eventually come home sober—or at least sober-ish. As a sixteen-year-old girl, I didn't have the gumption to hunt for them; calling around to police stations and hospitals was also unthinkable. If I caused my mother and her husband any trouble or embarrassment, I'd pay, so I didn't dare try.

Jumpy with adrenalin and apprehension, I busied myself by doing housework. A sparkling house might make my mother happy, and keeping her happy was a critical objective for me in those days. I started in the kitchen, removing all of the chipped, cracked, stained, and mismatched plates and glasses to wipe out the cabinets and re-thumbtack the paper liners. Then I pulled apart the stove to soak its crusty burners and scrub every white surface that was coated with amber-colored grease.

Next came the refrigerator. That relic had groaned and sputtered for years, causing milk to spoil, leftovers to get moldy, and meat to go rancid. When it would stop working, we discovered that if we held a lit match or two up to an exposed wire that ran between the interior thermostat dial and the upper icebox, the bipolar beast would chug back to life. The cost of a new refrigerator could have quickly been recouped in grocery bills, but since Food Stamps covered only food, not appliances, we made do. I worked like crazy for several hours, mopping the floor, dumping heaps of cigarette butts, and restacking piles of bills and papers that had no place to be filed.

It was close to ten o'clock that night when the phone finally rang—approximately thirty hours from when I had encouraged my mom to "Have fun," told her I loved her, and kissed her goodbye. It turns out, that was our final exchange. LG was at a hospital, and when I heard his voice, my first thought was, "Why is he calling?" In the thirteen years that he had been married to my mom, he and I had never spoken on the telephone.

And then, without any preface or attempt to soften the blow, he said, "Your mother is dead. I'll be home in about an hour."

When sober, LG's ability to communicate fell between silent scorn and expletive-laced commands, but this was different. His voice was devoid of emotion, flat, vacant. Perhaps he was in shock. Perhaps he actually said more, but I was in shock and stopped hearing at that point.

In fact, I didn't even ask what had happened. I didn't know if LG had killed my mother, or if she had fallen in a drunken stupor and hit her head, or what. All I could think in the moment was that he was coming home and she wasn't, and I was terrified. Without her to protect me from his rages, I didn't feel safe, and I literally didn't know how I was going to survive.

My mother had been incapable of shielding me from LG's verbal onslaughts, but when it came to physical ones, she had stepped in with the intensity of an angry mama bear. Only once did he ever get away with swiping at me. I had been jumping on the furniture, and he came after me with a yardstick, which he cracked across the back of my bare legs. I was six years old. He would have whacked me some more except the yardstick broke in half, and my mother jumped in. She told him that if he ever hit me again, it would be the last thing he would ever do since she would kill him—and we both believed her. But now, with her suddenly out of his way, I panicked at the thought that there might be ten years of pent-up blows he'd want to let loose.

He never did lay a hand on me after Mom died, but not a day went by when I wasn't afraid that he would. A couple of weeks after we buried Mom, I saw a copy of her death certificate. It said that she had a heart attack and had been dead on arrival at the hospital. So LG wasn't a murderer—but he wasn't a father to me either.

The day before my mother's funeral, LG's mother, Mrs. G, came to our house for the first time—ever. Mrs. G had never bothered to hide her low opinion of my mother, and refusing to grace our house with her presence was one of the ways she showed it.

A main cause for her scorn was the fact that my mother was a divorcée. When Mom was seventeen, she had married a fellow in the state of Arkansas. (That's where the name Ellis in those letters between the lawyers comes from.) A year into her marriage, in 1951, she gave birth to her first son, my oldest half brother, Gordon. But five years later, she filed for divorce. Her divorce decree, a document I found in the strongbox, reports on repeated beatings she endured from Ellis: he knocked her to the floor, against a wall, and out of a chair, and, to quote the document verbatim, "on or about March 7, 1956, defendant struck plaintiff repeated blows with his hands and fists, bruising her severely, and that on divers other occasions defendant has mistreated plaintiff and that all of such acts of defendant were without reason or provocation."

Either Mrs. G didn't know the circumstances of that first marriage, or she didn't care. Remarriage was a big, fat sin according to her. (It bears mentioning that LG had also been previously married. Apparently, his nuptials didn't count because Mrs. G had paid for an annulment.) She was also convinced that Mom had married LG for money, which meant *her* money, since LG himself was broke. Mrs. G did, on more than one occasion, pay our rent and put food on our table, but her help came at a high price. Every dollar was laced with spite and handed over begrudgingly. And then there were the stiff frowns that made it clear to anyone watching that I, the bastard daughter, would be tolerated, but the less Mrs. G saw of me, the better.

However, my mother did have one trump card over Mrs. G. When Mom gave birth to my half sister Ellie, Mrs. G had to decide whether to continue hating my mother and thereby forfeit a relationship with her only granddaughter or accept some kind of tacit peace. She chose the latter, and Ellie got the grandma treatment I didn't. Mrs. G fawned over her and showered her with gifts of velvet dresses, pony rides, special sugary treats, and extravagant toys. I was piqued by her obvious favoritism, but I realized that her disregard for me was also a strategic dig at my mother—the wicked, gold-digging divorcée.

When Mrs. G sat on the edge of a tattered couch in our living room that day before the funeral, nothing could have been more discomfiting to me—or her. The woman might as well have been the queen of England for how little she belonged in our run-down house. She certainly looked out of place with her fox-fur coat, leather gloves, and hair impeccably coiffed in a classic Grace Kelly French twist. I was so miserable that I slipped through a side door off of the kitchen and went to the backyard where I could wait out her bizarre visit. It was nearing the end of day, and the evening sky was heavy with fog. I hadn't thought to grab a sweater, but unwilling to participate in that theater of the absurd inside the house, I shivered from both raw nerves and a biting chill.

I had yet to shed any tears over my mother's death. Damp and unsettled, I sat down on the rusty seat plate of an old swing set that had been a leftover from the previous tenants of our rented house. The metal felt like ice through my blue jeans. With half-hearted effort, I kicked at the compacted dirt beneath my feet, shifting back and forth and from side to side. I wondered why I wasn't crying and assumed something was wrong with me. My grief didn't look or feel like anything I had seen on TV. None of my friends had dead mothers, and if there were any other students in my school who did, I didn't know about them.

In a way, my constipated tears were the result of suppressed emotions that had long predated my mother's death. I loved her, but I hated her alcoholism. Fresh in my mind were all of the days and nights when she would be either slumped over in a stupor or primed for a fight. In both cases, I made every effort to be invisible. I didn't want to wake her and have to contend with drunken nonsense, and if she was awake and angling for a row, I didn't want to become the target. My hair, my friends, the way I dressed, the way I spoke: anything could set her off, and once she was triggered, it would be a long night. By the time Mom died, I had no sympathy for the alcoholic.

But what about the woman? My feelings toward her weren't uncomplicated either. I had no doubt that she loved me, but to this day I can think of only one unadulterated expression of her caring. It was when I was four years old and had gotten my tonsils out. I remember being woken in the night and allowed to stay in my pajamas, even though we were getting in the car. I remember lying on a gurney in a brightly lit hospital corridor and Mom reluctantly letting go of my hand when a nurse came to wheel me into the operating room. After the surgery, I was brought back home and given a bedroom all to myself where my mother had put a small brass oriental gong next to the bed. If I needed anything, all I had to do was tap it. I tested the gong when everyone was asleep, and it worked; Mom came to my room without delay or annoyance. For a couple of days, I got ice cream, Jell-O, and orange-flavored

Aspergum. At no time during that period did I see my mother drunk. I trusted her to take care of me, and she did.

There were other times when mom was sober, and she became a different person then too. She'd say she was going on a diet, which generally meant she was giving up alcohol. She got out of bed earlier and changed out of her housecoat; conversation was lighter, and laughter more spontaneous; projects got started; meals were thoughtfully prepared; and the fighting between her and LG stopped. But those so-called diets didn't last more than a week or two, if that; inevitably, they would be drowned in the undertow of her alcoholism. And I knew how to tell which period she was in. When I would get home from school in the afternoon, as soon as I came through the door, my eyes would go directly to her glass. If the liquid was brown, it was diet soda; if it was clear, then it was vodka and water, and she'd be gone. Her body would be present and animated, but the mother I wanted was nowhere in sight.

Her drinking ultimately ruined even some of the better moments I remember. One Sunday, when the weather was bad and no one else was home, she read the book *Love Story* to me. Mom was a reader, but she had never done anything like that before. This time, though, she read to me cover to cover. We both were weeping at the end, especially at the line, "Love means not ever having to say you're sorry," though I suspect those words pierced her heart for much different reasons than they pierced mine.

Mom read beautifully, fluidly, putting emphasis in just the right places, never stumbling over or mispronouncing a word. I, however, just couldn't get the hang of reading, so I hated it. In school, my attempts to sound out the words phonetically caused my classmates to snicker and gave the teacher fits. I could hear her exasperation as she spoke over my mistakes, feeding me the correct pronunciations. Often I ended up with my head on my desk and in tears. But that afternoon with Mom, listening to the written word was an absolute treat. I was enraptured, and Mom took great pride in the fact that she believed I was mature enough to handle the adult content of the story, even though I was only about ten or eleven.

The only problem was, she started drinking her vodka halfway through the book, so by the end she was well on her way to being buzzed. That's when things went south. I didn't know back then what she was looking for—a sadder response to the ending? an in-depth analysis of the book? higher praise for her excellent reading?—and I still don't know. Whatever it was, my response hadn't been what she wanted, and she suddenly couldn't stand the sight of me. She ordered me to go to my room with one of her more common punishing phrases: "Get out of my sight." I retreated in shame, unsure of what I had done wrong or when it would be safe to reemerge.

That's how memories of my mother went: kernels of quality time alternating with boozy stretches, which would swamp whatever pleasure I might take from the recollection of the former. Christmases, birthdays, vacations, back-to-school nights, boy crushes, my first period: all conjured up memories that made me cringe. And those were the *good* times.

Regardless of Mom's moods, things were rough all around in our house. We were always hurting for money. There were years and years of unemployment for both her and LG. My clothes were mostly secondhand, and our furniture was even older and shabbier. Most of the time we didn't own a car. There were times when there really wasn't quite enough to eat. At one point, when we were living on Mrs. G's old ranch property, LG shot pigeons from the barn for our dinner. I remember plucking feathers and singeing the finer ones with a lit candle before the birds went into a soup pot. We got medical care only in the most urgent situations. Once when I came down with a case of impetigo on my face, it was allowed to develop until I looked so hideous that a neighbor finally took me to see her doctor. It was bleak.

When I hit adolescence and became more self-conscious, I began judging who I was based on the world around me, and I came up short—way short. I noticed that the atmosphere in my friends' homes was nothing like the one in mine. For one thing, there was a level of predictability that mine never had. And no one I knew ever seemed to be afraid that when they got home from school at the end of the day, they'd be walking into a drunken brawling fight between their parents.

I would have spent every night at someone else's house if I could. But as I put more and more sleepover requests to my mother, she just got resentful, and threatened that if I didn't like where I was living, maybe I should leave and not come back. There was an established understanding that home belonged to my parents. I was allowed to live there, but that privilege could be revoked any time. I was truly afraid of the door being locked against me, and if I didn't have a friend to take me in, I would literally be left out in the cold.

My mother's resentment wasn't about anything I had done wrong, or even about my not wanting to spend time with her and LG. Basically, she was annoyed by my attraction to the world outside. If she happened to be in a bad mood when I asked to go to a friend's house, her face would tighten with a ferocity that let me know I had really pissed her off. That look of piercing disdain would cut me to the quick. And not only would I have to stay home, I'd likely be subjected to a tirade about my audacity in wanting to branch out. Even if I could launch a defense, which I couldn't because I didn't have the words in my vocabulary, she wouldn't hear it. Her anger, especially when she was intoxicated, was unrelenting. My only defense was to blame myself. Instead of getting mad at LG or my mother, or railing against our sorry circumstances, I figured I must have done something wrong to have caused such contempt.

Another consequence for my emotional life is that I started lying to keep everyone in the dark about what was going on and how I felt. To appease my mother and not set her off, I downplayed what my friends had come to mean to me. To my friends, I would downplay how fraught my home life was. No one at that time had any clue that I was living with narcissistic, violent alcoholics. Eventually, I could no longer tell the difference between who I really was and who I was pretending to be. I was overwhelmed with a pervasive sense of being a fraud, as well as a deep fear of being shunned, so I tried harder and harder to control people's impressions of me. I would tell my friends, "I swear on a stack of Bibles" that I had the trendiest must-have toys at home but wasn't allowed to take them out, or that I had famous relatives who lived far away but sent me letters all the time. I had one kid believing that the comedian George Carlin was my uncle (why George Carlin is anyone's guess except he was popular and I knew his name.)

I understood that I was fibbing and it was wrong, but I did it anyway. Maintaining the charade was exhausting, of course, but I'd be damned if I was going to admit to my deceits. Still, my dishonesty further corroded what little self-esteem I had because now I felt guilty about what I was doing. I wasn't who I said I was. I was a phony, and if anyone caught on, there would be no recovering.

Thinking back, this particular incident encapsulates that burgeoning emotional state. It was a day that I begged my mother for a new pair of tennis shoes and promised I would take good care of them. The ones I was coveting reminded me of lemon meringue pie, with their yellow canvas and pristine white laces and rubber soles. When Mom agreed to buy them, I couldn't have been happier. I must have said thank you and told her that I loved her a hundred times on the way home.

The first thing I wanted to do was wear them to a friend's house to show off. To get there, I had to cross a cable-and-plank bridge that was strung across a seasonal creek that ran alongside the road. The problem was, it was the middle of winter, and it had been raining heavily for many days. The creek had turned into a frantic torrent, with opaque, mud-brown water crashing over boulders and slamming into the banks. The force of its current was enough to suck whole trees from the ground, and its roar was such that I was sure no one would hear me if anything happened and I had to scream for help. I had no interest in turning around and going home without modeling how special I was in my brand-spanking-new shoes, however. Frightened but determined, I ran across the bridge as fast as I could. But then, mid-span, a plank broke into two pieces, and my foot fell through. My momentum allowed me to hurl forward, but when I pulled my foot from the now-dangling plank, my shoe came off and was instantly consumed by the monstrous water below. My instinct was to jump in to retrieve it, but I knew better. My seventy-pound body was no match for those deadly rapids. I ran along the creek's edge hoping it would surface, but no; the brilliant yellow sneaker was gone.

When I arrived at my friend's house, limping with one shoe on and one shoe off, her mother was horrified to hear about my near disaster. I was horrified too, but not because of what might have happened to me; I was sick over losing my beautiful new shoe and petrified about the prospect of breaking the news to my mother. I had promised over and over to take extra special care of those shoes, and now I had already lost one. The fear of disappointing her had me in tears.

On some level, of course, my reaction wasn't that unusual. Many kids would be afraid to tell their parents they'd just lost something brand-new. What set me apart was just how infuriated my mother could get. It's striking that it never even occurred to me to be outraged that the bridge was so unsafe, or relieved that nothing worse had happened. My only reaction was to feel guilty. I assumed that my wanting to show off and my running had been reckless, and so I had gotten what I deserved. I didn't think, *This is bad*; I thought, *I am bad*. My friend's mother gave me a pair of her daughter's old shoes so that I could get home. There I was, back in castoffs—my self-assessed, pitiful lot in life. I don't recall my mother being as upset as I had feared she would be, but I do remember that we never went back to the store to get a replacement pair.

Guilt, shame, and fear of abandonment became a habit, or almost a kind of muscle memory. Fortunately, I seem to have also been blessed with certain positive qualities that kept me from completely succumbing to those debilitating emotions. I was clever, and from an early age, I had an undaunted, can-do attitude that helped me get some of my needs met. I was especially creative in how I got money. Before I was old enough to even babysit, I would go on concerted hunts to find stray cash. It was surprising to me how many people wouldn't retrieve their change from pay phones and vending machines. In Laundromats, I would find and straighten a wire hanger to scoop out all of the lint and debris from under the washers and dryers; almost always there would be a few nickels, dimes, or quarters in the catch. I only outright stole money from one person, LG. He had a habit of jangling coins in his pockets, so early in the morning, when I could hear that both he and my mother were sound asleep, I would sneak into their room and slip my hand into his trousers that were lying on a chair. My little fingers could gauge what denomination I was lifting by its size and the roughness or smoothness of its edge. I hunted for the quarters.

As I got older, I did a lot of babysitting, yard work, and housekeeping. One December, my brother and I packaged up pounds of mistletoe and sold it around the neighborhood. By Christmas, Sean and I had made enough money for him to buy a brand-new Bianchi ten-speed bicycle and for me to amass fifty dollars. Eventually I was buying most of my own clothes and treating myself to outings with friends. By the time my mother died, I think I had more money saved up than she did. I didn't dare brag about it, though. I would have been accused of thinking I was better than her. "Who in the hell do you think you are?" was a question I knew well.

But there was something else that kept me going during this rough time: the idea that my biological father was out there somewhere and would someday come and save me. At the very least, the idea that I *had* a real father made me feel like the life I was living wasn't my real life; *that* was somewhere else. My mother never sat me down and explained who that man was or how she had come to (possibly) have two children with him. But I thought it must be Mr. Abbott because of the way she would occasionally mention him and wistfully declare, "I worshiped the ground that man walked on." That was enough for me, and I pretty much ran with it from there and created a person I could worship the same way.

I culled bits of information about him and massaged them into a character who was admirable and sympathetic. Some of my ideas came from snatches of conversation I overheard when my mother would drunk-dial her few distant friends and talk to them late into the night. But in the end, I simply made up most of his personal profile.

The one thing I did know about Mr. Abbott was that he was married to someone else, and that he and his wife had other children. So I decided that he must have been Catholic and therefore prohibited by the church from getting divorced. I also decided that he was Sean's father too, because of my mother's four children, he and I look the most alike.

In cinematic Technicolor, I envisioned a passionate but secret romance between Mr. Abbott and my beautiful, young mother, while his wife I cast in the role of an unforgiving, possessive shrew. I turned his legitimate children into snotty-nosed, spoiled brats. I devised a home life for him that was immaculate yet unbearable. He was a stoic gentleman who bore the grief of his lost love in private shame and sorrow. My mother was his forbidden fruit, and theirs was a love that would never die, yet, tragically, could not go on. Alas, the day had come when, in a grand heroic gesture, he had had to turn from my mother so that she could live the life she deserved, outside the shadows of deceit.

How fine a gentleman I created. With every offense LG committed, I imagined my father doing the opposite. When LG licked his dinner plate clean, I pictured my father in a satin-lapelled dinner jacket, slicing filet mignon with the finest silver flatware. While LG's greatest accomplishment for the day was watching television, my father was an astronaut, a brain surgeon, or a briefcase-carrying businessman. LG was short; my father must have been tall. LG was cruel, so I imagined my father kind. LG was near penniless, so Dad must have been fiscally fit. On the morning when LG—much to my horror—let his bathrobe fall open to air out his genitals, I imagined that my biological father never possessed those hideous appendages. Without any evidence to the contrary, I believed LG could do no right while my distant daddy could do no wrong.

Another thing that burnished Mr. Abbott's image in my mind was the ninety-dollar checks that arrived from him each month. Since he and my mother had never been married, he didn't *have to* send that money, I figured. He did it just because he was nice. He was our morally righteous secret benefactor. Even when the checks mysteriously stopped coming a few months before Sean turned eighteen and I was fifteen, I clung to my fantasy. He couldn't just be stiffing us; there had to have been a good reason for his actions.

In my need to rationalize, I went so far as to conclude that Sean and I were something truly special. I knew we were illegitimate, but because of the inviolability of our parents' clandestine love, and the fact that Mr. Abbott never seemed to be the object of my mother's acerbic temper, we were somehow *better* than my two half siblings. For many years that worked to buoy my flagging self-esteem. In fact, my childish construct gave me a level of confidence that I'm convinced saved my life. It fed the part of my ego that tells me that I matter and I'm worth fighting for.

But sitting on the swing set that day before my mother's funeral, those positive feelings were nowhere in evidence. Not that I was grieving. I tried to make myself cry, telling myself, *I'm so sad. I'm so sad,* but a different thought was far more insistent: *What am I going to do?* Without my mother, my future with LG was horrible to contemplate. My mother was an alcoholic, but she was also my protector. With her gone, there was nothing to shield me from LG's wrath. He had made it abundantly clear over the years that he was not responsible for "those bastards." Maternally orphaned and paternally abandoned, I had no contingency plan to fall back on, and I was terrified. Amidst those thoughts, LG came around the corner and found me.

"Get in the goddamn house and show my mother some respect," he barked.

T hings didn't change much with LG during the next year, but I was underage and had no place to go, so I just had to wait it out. LG still worked at the bar and often came home drunk. I would hear his key in the door at around three o'clock in the morning, followed by a lot of slamming around. He'd crash into tables and chairs, turn on the television, bang the kitchen cupboards, drop glasses, and cuss when they shattered. He would open my bedroom door, and while I pretended to be asleep, he'd stand there and mumble incoherently—disjointed, incomplete sentences that included ugly words of hate: whore, bastard, bitch, cunt, and slut. These breathy tirades included demands that I get out of his house and not come back. Perhaps he was hoping I would respond, but I stayed perfectly still, controlling my breath so that it sounded heavy with sleep. Sober the next day, he'd be withdrawn but civil, as if nothing unusual had happened.

One afternoon, he totally shocked me by starting an actual conversation—a first. Typically, our exchanges had been brief and to the point. I'd ask him for money to go buy groceries or I'd tell him where Ellie was; he'd tell me to move out of the way of the television or to get off the damn telephone. I wasn't curious about him, and he wasn't curious about me.

When he cleared his throat and began talking, my initial thought was that this was going to be the day when he would tell me to hit the road. Instead, he unloaded the details of what had happened on the day my mother died. He wasn't drunk; still, his speaking to me like this was enough to send my heart rate soaring. The lead-in was something like, "I need to talk to you," and it freaked me out to be addressed in an adult manner instead of being scolded like a child.

He said that he and Mom had stayed all night and most of the next day at his bar. When they left, they went to a popular hot dog place on San Pablo Avenue. They took their food over to the Berkeley Marina, parked along the water, ate, and enjoyed the sun setting across the bay. I could see every detail as he described it. I could well imagine his sloppy driving and their besotted ambling. He didn't say that they fought, although it wouldn't have surprised me if they had. They were no longer throwing punches, but their current dance was to argue and get under each other's skin.

He then explained that it looked as if Mom had fallen asleep. She was drunk, and he thought she had simply passed out. At one point he tried to wake her, but she didn't respond. He said that he shook her and yelled her name, but there was nothing. He thought he could get to the hospital faster than he could find a pay phone or get an ambulance, so he started driving. Her death certificate indicated that she was dead on arrival, and the cause was "cardiac failure" due to "arteriosclerotic heart disease."

LG's face twisted into a grimace of torment as he recalled the events of that night. His bloodshot eyes didn't focus on me or what was right in front of him; they roamed around the living room, seeming to search for some clue that would undo the hard fact of Mom's death. Perhaps he thought that in the telling he would locate some missing detail that could absolve him of his role. He hadn't killed her, but he hadn't saved her either. Near the end of LG's revealing account, he asked me if he had done anything wrong.

Oddly, I didn't think he was asking for forgiveness so much as condemnation. Placing blame on something, even himself, was better than the tetherless state he was in. In love and war, Mom had been his anchor, his north star. She had accepted him for better and for worse, and without her, he teetered closer to the edge than I had ever realized was possible. On him, grief and heartbreak didn't look like sadness; it looked like wild-eyed desperation.

For years, I had felt nothing but fear and loathing toward this man, so you might think this would have been my chance for revenge—to condemn him to a lifetime of guilt. But I found I couldn't do it. My mother had a hand in her death too. It was their lifestyle; suicidal drinking was what they did. Also, LG was in such a state that I wondered if he was thinking about killing himself. For the first time in my life, I actually felt sorry for him. Also, I figured he needed to keep it together for Ellie, because when I was gone, he would be all she had. So I told him no, I didn't think her dying was his fault.

After that, I just kept going to school and working, trying not to attract any unwanted attention from LG. But I suffered another blow a few months later when my gramma died. Well, she wasn't my real grandmother; she was my best friend's grandmother, but not having a grandparent of my own, she had become like one to me. In fact, Gramma had been my safe haven. As an elderly woman living alone (her husband had died young in a workplace explosion), she did what she could for me. She marveled at my pluck and independence, and she praised my skill and ability to work hard around her house and yard. She was nothing but complimentary to me. When I'd grocery shop for her, she'd swoon over the fresh produce I had picked or the sale items I had discovered. When we talked, she hung on my every word. She was unwavering in her affection, and I cherished every minute with her.

I was sad when she died, but by this point in my life, I had jettisoned so many feelings of grief that I was no longer capable of feeling much of anything. As I did when my mother died, I just became numb, as emotionally shut down as I could be while still able to function.

Meanwhile, I was making plans to move out, and they were starting to pick up. As it was, my best friend from high school, Susan, was also eager to be out on her own, and she worked like I did, so she, too, had some money. She was good at searching the classifieds and want ads, and when she found a two-bedroom duplex for rent that we could afford, we decided to inquire.

I had to lie about my age (I was five months shy of my eighteenth birthday) and my job situation on the application. At the time, I was babysitting for a woman who was a biologist, so I called myself a "student aid," thinking it sounded more mature and trustworthy. We got lucky that the owners didn't call any of our references, and at the end of a brief face-to-face meeting, they gave us a set of keys to the Cleveland Street duplex.

The place was small and run-down and not in the best of neighborhoods. It was under the freeway, across the street from the train tracks, and within sight and smell of the brackish tidal waters of the bay. But we thought it was fabulous. It was dry, it had electricity and running water, it was near a bus stop, and it was affordable. When the owners drove off, Susan and I hugged and squealed like the young girls we were, incredulous at our score.

Susan waited to move in until the exact date she turned eighteen and could leave home legally, but I didn't care about that. I was so done with LG by that time that I moved those several months before turning eighteen, almost a year to the day after my mother died. But the truth is, I remember almost nothing about the actual day I left home. I can't say which clothes I took or what I left behind. I don't recall if I used a suitcase, a box, or grocery bags to hall my belongings. I couldn't say if it was day or night, weekday or weekend. I don't even know if I took the bus or had a friend drive me. I do know that I had kept LG and Ellie, who was twelve at the time, in the dark about my plans, and didn't say goodbye or leave a note. And I know that I took a pocket-sized diary that my mother had given me when I turned thirteen because I still have it. Birds and flowers adorn its cover, and the very first entry describes, in undisciplined penmanship and disastrous grammar, a day when I fretted about my mother. In part, I had written, " . . . she think eather dady hert her or a broken rib." ("Dady" refers to LG.) I couldn't leave that unguarded observation behind.

I also know that my memory lapse had nothing to do with rage. When I walked out on Ellie and her father I had reached a point where I wasn't so much mad as I was done. I wasn't going to let the two of them call me a bastard one more time. It was a word LG had used with great satisfaction through-out my childhood to enflame my mother—a power play that escalated their every argument. His ace insult found its target in me before my overhearing young ears even knew what it meant. Once my mother was gone, my little sister found the nerve to start mimicking her father and calling me a bastard too. "No, I don't have to go to school. I don't have to listen to you. You're not my mommy; you're a bastard."

I was done—and ready to move on. And even though the Cleveland Street duplex was my ninth address (my family had moved a lot), the process of transplanting didn't scare me. It was simple: find another place, pack, unpack, and adjust. Bonding with people, places, and things was the luxury of another class of folk. But there was one big difference this time: unlike all the other moves, this one involved true hope for change.

I had told only one person about my plans to run away from home. Mr. B was the head counselor at my high school, but I knew him better from working as his house cleaner for the past year.

Mr. B was a widower raising three kids on his own, and he was nothing like the other adult male in my life. Compared to everyone I knew, in fact, he seemed incredibly balanced; he was irreverent without being cynical, confident without being arrogant, funny without being clownish. He exuded levity, and his demeanor conveyed the message that things would turn out okay and not to worry. He also had a lot of friends whom he loved to entertain, which fascinated me. It's no exaggeration to say that LG did not have a single friend, and no one ever visited him and my mother at our house. So I had very little practice interacting with adults. But that didn't stop Mr. B from treating me like one.

While I was dusting, he would tell me lively, detailed stories of what he'd heard or experienced. He didn't curse or raise his voice or speak of women in a disrespectful way, and he would always pause long enough to see if I wanted to interject a thought of my own. I usually didn't—I was so nonplussed by the experience of being talked *to*, not *at*—and when I did, my response was often something along the lines of "Oh, wow," or "How cool."

When my mom died, Mr. B may have noticed my distracted demeanor, but he didn't come out point-blank and ask if I was okay. I guess one doesn't become the head counselor of a large urban high school without knowing a thing or two about teenagers. I felt that losing one's mother at such a young age was weird, and that, in turn, translated into *my* being weird. I had always wanted to be invisible even before my mother's untimely death, but after it, any sign of difference between me and the other kids was downright excruciating. I couldn't stand being looked at or probed about my feelings, and Mr. B seemed to understand that.

Honestly, though, the main reason I told Mr. B about leaving home was that I knew he would get wind of it soon enough, and I was concerned that he might have a professional obligation to inform school district administrators of my status as a minor without adult supervision. But I was methodical enough in my details that I won him over. I explained about the duplex that Susan and I had rented. I told him that I would be dropping out of high school and that I intended to enroll in cosmetology school.

I'm sure I put him in an uncomfortable position, but he was supportive, and he saw that this was a viable option for a student who had few. He didn't rat me out, and truant officers never came looking for me.

Nor did LG—not that he could have found me if he'd wanted to. LG knew that I worked, but he had no idea where. He knew I had friends, but he didn't know their last names and had no way of getting their phone numbers. That meant I could hide in plain sight.

Susan and I made a good team, full of moxie and never doubting our ability to succeed. And we complemented each other in our differences. Intellectually, she was light years ahead of me. She was always reading from newspapers, magazines, and books, and she could speak in depth on topics that I knew little or nothing about: Rastafarians, the IRA, Édith Piaf, the Holocaust, Sung Myung Moon and the Moonies, Watergate, and so on. She could say thank you in French,

Spanish, and Japanese. While I was drooling over John Travolta in *Saturday Night Fever*, she had discovered Akira Kurosawa films. We both wanted to get out of high school early, so we took the General Equivalency Diploma test, and she passed. I failed it twice before giving up.

I, on the other hand, had plenty of seat-of-the-pants knowledge. My mother had trained me young how to run a household. I could plan meals, cook, and clean. I could pay bills, balance a checkbook, fix a leaking faucet and sew clothes, and I was a fiend at saving money. (I still had almost all of the Social Security death benefit checks I had received from the government when my mother died.)

Susan appreciated all of that and, most importantly, never made me feel inferior. Quite the opposite. She exposed me to all sorts of ideas and activities. With her, I discovered the differences between polyester and cashmere, Velveeta cheese and Camembert, Reno and Monaco. She took me to my first rock concert—Elton John—exposing me to all of his over-the-top, theatrical musical genius and glory. Together, we didn't go thrift shopping so much as treasure hunting. Susan always had a keen eye for the most valuable merchandise hidden amongst piles of junk. Just being with her helped me to ignore my memories of being a flea-bitten, rag-wearing, Welfare-receiving bastard.

But they didn't always stay away. At one point, Susan and I bought brand-new, top-of-the-line roller skates, which we'd ride everywhere. Often we'd tool around UC Berkeley, where I was reminded of the vast differences between us. Susan felt completely at home in this environment, but I didn't know a single person who had gone to college. It was nothing I even remotely aspired to. I admired the grounds and the grand architecture of the school, but it was like visiting a foreign country where I knew nothing of the customs, culture, or language.

It didn't really matter, though, because of my beauty-school plan. So I continued working at my ordinary jobs until it was time to enroll. Mornings and mid-afternoons I cashiered at a local doughnut shop, and in the later afternoons I continued with Mr. B's house a few hours per week and my "student aid" job—cooking, cleaning, and babysitting for the biologist, a single mother with full custody of her two boys.

Athena Beauty College, as a purveyor of beauty, left plenty to be desired, but it was almost free, and it provided the nineteen hundred hours of training that I needed for the California Board of Cosmetology licensing exam. The student body was a mixture of men and women, gay and straight, young and old, and included many ethnicities and socioeconomic classes. There were aspiring hairdressers but also a fair number of rudderless drifters: prostitutes, drug addicts, alcoholics, and schemers of various kinds.

The place itself was also on the shabbier side. There was a front door and a back door but no windows to open. Pot smoking in the bathroom wasn't uncommon, and the patrons were allowed to smoke while having their hair done. (The chairs still had those built-in ashtrays.) It was a wonder the place didn't spontaneously combust from the fumes of marijuana, nicotine, hair spray, peroxide and ammonia in the hair dye, sodium hydroxide in the chemical relaxers, ammonium thioglycolate in the permanent waves, perfume, cologne, and un-deodorized body odor. Walking outside, it was possible to detect the school by smell from a hundred yards away.

There was never any roll call; the staff couldn't have cared less whether I showed up or not. And it was up to me how quickly I would accumulate the nineteen hundred hours needed to finish the program. It was possible to graduate in nine months, but I had to maintain my various income-earning jobs, so my training took almost two years.

We started out by working on mannequins, but it wasn't long before we were able to practice on "live" patrons. People could get their hair washed for fifty cents or cut and styled for seventy-five. Hair coloring, permanent waves, and straightening were more expensive but still a fraction of what professionals charged. Those low prices brought in a clientele of the very young, the very old, and the very cheap. Yes, it's true that if you tip ten cents on a fifty-cent service, it's a twenty percent tip, but it still felt kind of humiliating. I learned how to accept tips graciously, though. In fact, I learned more about how to maintain professional composure than I did about how to cut and style hair. And it was invaluable training.

Without groaning or gasping, I was expected to do scalp inspections before every hairdressing service, and there were many times when I'd have to swallow hard before putting my hands on heads. Strange growths, dents, and scales were not uncommon. There was a regular coterie of little old ladies who came in for shampoos and sets once or twice a month and didn't wash their hair between appointments. My ability to disassociate came in handy during these encounters. It wasn't the healthiest coping strategy, but it sure helped me cultivate professionalism at work. Most of the time, anyway.

One day, one of my little sister's playmates came in with her father for a haircut. I was disoriented at first, since it had been a year since I'd seen them, but the girl knew me immediately and hugged me like an old friend. "How are you?" we asked simultaneously. It was then that she told me that Ellie had been put in foster care. The news hit me like a jolt of electricity. Ellie had been LG's pride and joy, his most cherished love. He would have done anything in his power for her. If she wanted to stay home from school to be with him, she could. If she wanted candy for dinner, he gave it to her. She could sit on his lap, and she could make him laugh out loud. With her, he was a different man. So any kind of rift between them signaled some kind of disaster.

I finally recovered my senses enough to ask what had happened, but all the girl said was, "Her dad snapped."

Before they left, I asked them if they could give me a phone number where Ellie was living. I phoned her as soon as I could that same day. More than a year had passed since we had spoken or seen each other. The pitch of my little sister's voice shot up with excitement when she heard me on the other end. There was no hint of resentment or anger, and she never questioned why I had left. But she was oddly blasé about her circumstances. I got the sense that she was experiencing foster care as if it were an extra-long sleepover. In fact, she appeared to like where she was and didn't express any interest in going home.

Ellie and I set a time for me to come visit the next Sunday. As soon as I arrived, she wanted to show me her new bedroom, a room she shared with another of the many foster children who were living in the house. As we passed through the kitchen, I spied my mother's cedar loveseat, an unmistakable piece of furniture that had belonged to her father. It was as close to a multigenerational family heirloom that we had. I stopped dead at the sight of it. I couldn't understand how this foster woman had come in contact with my sister or my mother's belongings. I wondered what else she had helped herself to.

I asked about it, and the woman's response was something along the lines of, "That old thing? We took it when we got Ellie. It's all going to be thrown away when the eviction goes through." Her dismissive attitude made me want to scratch her eyes out. Just because I had turned away from everything didn't mean that it was valueless. The whole encounter also felt like a way of trivializing my dead mother.

I couldn't find the words to say how double-crossed I felt.

But I didn't want Ellie to feel bad, and since I didn't know what had landed her in foster care, maybe I wasn't even right about everything. I just knew that Ellie's foster mother was arrogant and condescending, and she stirred up all kinds of painful feelings in me about LG, my mother, my childhood, and everything else. I couldn't get out of that house fast enough. I noticed a flash of disappointment in Ellie's eyes when I claimed to have someplace else to go, but it quickly disappeared. We were both masters at hiding our emotions, especially the ones that hurt. I promised that I would call and see her again, but I had little intention of doing either any time soon. In our goodbye embrace, we both said that we loved each other, but it sounded feeble. She and her foster mother stood at the front door until I drove off, each of us waving and smiling with our individual degrees of false enthusiasm.

I still couldn't believe this had happened, so I decided to go to LG's house to see if I could find out anything more. As I approached, I could tell that something was seriously amiss. The place looked abandoned. The grass was waist-high with foxtails and thistles, and there were leaves, garbage, and faded newspapers clustered against the side fence. One of the six panes in the living room window was fractured in a spider web pattern. I had been apprehensive about this return from the start, but the horror of what I was looking at kept me pinned inside the car. I still had a key to the house, but I wasn't sure if I had the nerve to use it. But I knew that this was going to be my one and only chance, and I had to take it.

Rattled through and through, I made myself proceed—and the horrors intensified. On the landing of the porch I saw the cold, charred remains of a fire. Within the cinders and ash were the blackened bones of a small animal, possibly a kitten.

But even that didn't prepare me for what I found inside. My hands flew up to my face to protect my nose from the stench. It was frightening, but I felt compelled to bear witness to the extent of LG's collapse.

Looking beyond the clutter and filth, there were two sites that shocked me the most. At the first, hundreds of holes had been drilled into the living room wall in the shape of a fireplace. I couldn't imagine what that was about. The other was our fifty-gallon fish tank. The aquarium had been shattered, releasing a tidal wave of water, tropical fish, decorative pebbles, coral chunks, plastic sea palms, and a miniature ceramic treasure chest and sunken ship. The flood had soaked the wall-to-wall carpet, which caused long-forgotten birdseed to sprout into a mat of grass. The water had since evaporated, and the fescue had folded over and died. Captured in relief in that web of dead sprouts were the skeletal remains of freshwater fish.

The broader disorder included the wooden coffee table, which had dozens of burn marks where cigarette butts had been stubbed out, plates of crusty, unrecognizable food, broken knickknacks, and helter-skelter hardware and hand tools. There were scattered piles of mail, newspapers, phonebooks, paper bags, and wads of rags. Kitty litter had been dumped in piles and shamelessly utilized by the cat. I moved to the kitchen where there was more evidence of fire. The white enameled backsplash of our 1950s-era stove was as black as its cast-iron burners, and soot covered the walls. The bathroom was also a disaster zone. The medicine cabinet mirror was broken to pieces. The shower curtain was torn and stained with black mold. The toilet was leaking and had buckled the floor. And the cat had used the towels and clothes on the floor for a litter box.

I had to get out of that hellscape. It wasn't my home anymore. It wasn't even the home of an extreme alcoholic; it was the dwelling of a madman. At that point I went from panic to full-throttle terror. I was afraid that the lunatic would come through the door and catch me prowling his den of psychosis. But before I escaped, a thought came to me as a clear directive: "Get Mom's strongbox, and run!"

When I arrived back home I was shaken, but I had made it out and was back in the safety of my little duplex. Alone in my room, I spent some time looking into the contents of the strongbox. I was curious but cautious. It didn't matter that my mother was dead and gone; she still had a powerful hold over me. I imagined that she would have been livid to see me prying into her past. I was trespassing on her private possessions, and I feared some kind of karmic retribution. It was as if the box had etched across the top, "Enter at your own risk."

The first thing I saw inside was a King James Bible, the kind sold by door-to-door salesmen back in the days of Fuller Brush men and Avon ladies. The thick book no longer had a cover on it, and the outside pages were stained, tattered, or altogether missing. I had to wonder if it was a vestige of some former self: my mother as a young woman before the warping effects of daily drinking turned her cynical and distrustful. Tucked into the Holy Book's pages were two envelopes, one with "Sean's Hair" written on it in my mother's handwriting, and the other, torn apart with half missing, with a few letters of "Terry's First Haircut" on it. Both packets held strands of our flaxen hair, soft as angora.

I also found a copy of my mother's divorce decree from Gordon's father. I couldn't comprehend its legalese, but I knew from the whispered comments my mother had made about him that he was nobody I'd want to know. Checks never came in the mail from Eugene Ellis, nor were birthday cards or letters addressed to Gordon. When Gordon was nineteen, he went to meet his father and came back traumatized by the experience. It was the 1960s, and Gordon had long hair. He said that his father took him to some local redneck bar where his dad and his dad's friends pinned him down and cut off his ponytail; then they stole his money and told him to get out of town. He had to hitchhike back to California. When I saw the divorce decree, all I could think was, "Thank God *he* wasn't my father."

There were other enigmatic legal docs that I didn't even try to pick my way through. Moving on, I found a few school portraits from years past and a couple of Ellie's report cards. There was a wooden cigar box crammed with slips of ephemera: a movie stub, a dry cleaners tag, pawn tickets and layaway slips, paycheck stubs, and the like—nothing I felt compelled to analyze at the time. There were a couple of yellow Kodak envelopes that held several photo negatives, but I couldn't make out what or who they were pictures of.

Then I discovered my birth certificate. It said my name was Terry Sue Ellis. I was incredulous, but I flat-out rejected the possibility that it was accurate. Further down the page, my father's name was listed as Gerrick Abbott Ellis. These names did not mesh with my understanding. There was a Gerrick Abbott and a Eugene Ellis, but there was no such person named Gerrick Abbott Ellis. From the time I was in kindergarten and learned my letters and how to write my name, I used LG's last name—Terry Sue G—because my mother had been married to him. To learn that my official last name was Ellis made my head spin. I didn't believe it! Gordon and I were half siblings, *had* to be. I had spent years secretly musing that I was an Abbott, and I wasn't going to let go of that. I didn't care what the stupid old birth certificate said.

With that disturbing revelation, I did what I always did when life got unpleasant; I shut off my brain and carried on as if nothing was bothering me. Whatever the strongbox had to reveal, I wasn't ready for it. I put the contents back inside and tucked the metal box into a corner of my closet, much the same way it had been tucked into the corner of my mother's closet. Whatever was in there would have to wait.

I came into contact with LG for the last time several months after I had bolted from his house. He showed up at Athena Beauty College looking for me. The reception area was clogged with waiting customers, and I was at my styling station pinning plastic curlers into the hair of a white-haired old lady.

I looked up and saw a disheveled transient walking straight toward me. He was ratty-haired and bearded, and he was wearing oil-stained, threadbare polyester pants, no shirt but a denim jacket open to the waist. He was barefoot, his feet crusted with street filth and his uncut toenails outlined in black grime. He was holding out a bouquet of calla lilies, clutching their long green stems with a hand as soiled as his feet. The flowers had clearly been plucked from some yard; moist black dirt was clinging to their bulbs and trailing roots. He thrust the floral offering at me without saying a word. His expression was a mixture of amusement at my extreme discomfort, haughty pride for the audience he had generated, and wild desperation.

"LG, you can't stay here. I can't talk to you right now," I said with as much calm as I could muster. I didn't want the situation to escalate; I just wanted him to leave. He held his place for a prolonged moment, assessing me in my tidy white smock and pressed blue slacks. The white-haired woman in my chair was frozen by the distressing proximity of this aberrant beast of a man. I had to break his spell. "LG, you have to leave," was all I could think to say. Our eyes were locked; it was a face-off of wills. His piercing gaze intensified, and it felt like the very essence of my being was skewered by his appraisal. From his penetrating stare, he was saying, "I know you, you bastard."

That was all he had, his top card, his power play, and this time I didn't flinch. In my mind, I knew I wasn't what he thought of me. He was the broken one, not me. Unable to secure his psychic prey, he relented. His squint relaxed, the muscles in his face softened, and without saying a single word, he turned around and walked away.

I threw the lilies into the nearest waste receptacle and went back to setting the old lady's hair.

That encounter settled nothing. It was the first time that I was able to get LG to back off before anything escalated, but I had no confidence that he wouldn't return. Ironically, what probably saved me from another LG visitation was the fact that Athena Beauty College suddenly closed down, with very little warning. I still had a couple hundred more hours to complete before I could apply for the State Board Exam, and the nearest cosmetology school was in Walnut Creek, so another student and I hooked up to commute together. LG was never going to find me in Walnut Creek, so that was a relief, but the new pressure was that I had to quit all of my jobs to accommodate my new commute schedule. I had just enough money saved to stop working for the couple of months that it would take me to finish my training. But that meant I had to have faith that the whole beauty-college trip was going to get me somewhere; otherwise, I would have sacrificed a lot of time and money for nothing.

Scared? Yes. Petrified? Not exactly, because there was simply no choice. I was in too deep to allow myself to fail.

On my last day of beauty college, I received a certificate for having "satisfactorily completed the prescribed course of study in BEAUTY CULTURE." But I still had to pass the licensing test, and one statistic that was going around back then had me plenty worried. Comparing the number of people who signed up to go to beauty school with the number who eventually worked as a beautician for more than one year, someone had concluded that a person had a one in ten thousand chance of making hairdressing her life's profession. Still, that meant that if I could go the distance, then I wouldn't have much competition, and that could mean great job security. Glass half-full!

The crucial part of the State Board Exam, the teachers at both schools I attended had said, was hair coloring. Hair coloring is nothing like painting a wall in a house; what you see is not what you get. A brunette going blonde for the first time is different from a blonde needing a retouch at the roots. Tinting hair darker does not involve the same sectioning that lightening hair does. Roots that are half an inch long are handled differently from roots that are more than an inch long, and so on. This part of the test held the highest score, so if we flunked it, then we wouldn't be granted a license no matter how well we did on every other aspect of the exam.

It didn't start well. I flipped over my laminated card to see what type of color application I was going to have to execute, only the description didn't look like anything I had been taught. And my reading wasn't good enough to allow me to figure it out. Frantic, but wanting to appear cool, I did what I had always done on tests; I guessed.

We were given a bowl of shaving cream to represent the hair dye and do a mock application. A few minutes after I started applying the cream, the proctor suggested that I reread my card. I felt my cosmetology license slipping away, but for some reason I decided that the proctor was only trying to test my resolve. She wanted to see if I could handle myself under pressure, so I continued with the application. When she came around a second time, though, she picked up the card and read it aloud to me. I understood immediately that I was doing the wrong application. I had the white foam smeared all over the wrong part of my model's hair. The bell rang, and time was up. There was no time to fix my mistake.

This is exactly the kind of experience that would trigger the old demons, and sure enough, a bloom of self-hate destroyed my concentration. Some nasty, defeatist inner voice started telling me that I had some nerve thinking that I could be anything more than a babysitter or a house cleaner for the rest of my life. My destiny was locked in, and I was a fool to think that I might be a licensed professional with a clientele one day. The world of style and fashion was not for me, never had been, and never would be. Go home, and don't come back!

And home wasn't Cleveland Street: it was Mom and LG; it was poverty and chaos. It was as if some judge from Hell had sprung to life to tell me this one thing: "Get back where you belong."

Fortunately, the plucky, "don't-get-in-my-way" side of my personality reasserted itself and allowed me to silence that demonic voice. I told the proctor I was sorry, and that I now realized what I should have been doing. I asked if failing this part of the test meant that I would fail the entire thing, and if so, shouldn't I just excuse myself right now? The woman did not appear to be moved by the quiver in my voice, but she told me to keep going, so I soldiered on for the remainder of the day, resigned to the fact that even if I failed, I could retake the test as many times as I had to as long as I was willing to keep paying for it.

At the end of the day, once all our scores had been tabulated, the proctor returned with our results and called out, one by one, the names of those who had passed. As the number of recipients grew, I became fixated on the remaining certificates in the proctor's hand and the number of stylists still in the room. I could see that a few of us had not passed.

But then she called out my name, and the ordeal was over. I was in. When I put my trembling hand out to accept the certificate, the proctor held on to the slip of paper just long enough for me to look into her eyes. When I did, she gave me an encouraging wink and a smile. I'll never forget that woman. I was sure that I could do the work, but I also knew that my misstep had been critical, and that she had contributed a lot to my clutch victory. I was elated.

My next step was to find a beautician job.

There were many possibilities in the beauty business. One of the most adventurous would have been to join the salon staff on a cruise ship. I thought about all of the exotic places I could see and people I would meet, but then I realized that the ship's salon would most certainly cater to older women wanting roller sets—those fluff and bluff, lacquered antigravity marvels of a rapidly passing era—so I let that one go. There was Supercuts, which would have given me volumes of quickie-cut experience, but their pay was notoriously low. I also considered San Francisco, where a number of swank salons offered apprenticeship programs: Vidal Sassoon, Yosh, Paul Brown, I. Magnin. Established hairdressers in those places could make thousands of dollars a month in commissions and tips, but then I wondered if it was ever possible for a newbie like myself to rise through the ranks in those boutique salons. Furthermore, some of the trendiest places were also some of the most pretentious. I had one beauty school friend who was denied a position when she refused to change her name from Karen to Brook.

The more I thought about it, the more anxious and insecure I became—like the way I felt when I was convinced I'd blown the licensing exam. My inner naysayer started wagging a smart little finger at my every tentative aspiration, telling me more about why a particular job *wouldn't* work for me than why it would, and convincing me I wasn't worthy of the better-sounding positions. Luckily, though, my trusty roommate came to the rescue. Susan was the one who found the ad for Alexander Pope Haircutters in Berkeley, and when she described the job, it sounded perfect. What appealed to me most was that it was an entry-level position, which meant that my employer would have an opportunity to witness my exact skill level. I wouldn't have to pretend to know more than I did. Nothing feeds my pug-nosed, finger-wagging internal brat like pretending to be something that I'm not. She knows the difference. Full disclosure causes her to shrink back into her murky womb, where I wish she'd stay.

The next day I put on some of my trendiest clothes—white sailor pants and a vintage navy-blue Elizabeth Arden jacket—and went determined to convey enthusiasm without sounding like a dingbat.

One of the owners called me back for a second interview and asked me to bring a model to demonstrate my haircutting skills. I recruited a friend's little sister and decided to go for broke by giving her a radical change. The haircut was called a shake, which was different from a shag. It was heavily layered and brushed forward. I had never done one before, but I knew all of the elements involved. It was touch-and-go for a while—the cut was above the shoulder in length, and my model started out with hair halfway down her back—but it worked out in the end, and I got the job.

Arriving at work everyday was like going to a New York theater where I had a prime seat and backstage pass. The players, The Alexander Pope Haircutters, were former graduates or instructors from Vidal Sassoon Academy, so they were all gifted artists. I paid attention to how they cut hair and how they interacted with the clients. Sometimes they were flirty; sometimes they were silent and focused. In general, there was good-natured banter about music, movies, travel, restaurants, current affairs, and family affairs. And throughout the day, I was able to witness one marvelous transformation after another.

When the workday was over, all the new assistants would get hands-on instruction from the haircutters, which meant I was essentially getting Vidal Sassoon–caliber training without having to pay the thousands of dollars it would cost to attend a Vidal Sassoon Academy. I admired my teachers tremendously. They really wanted us to succeed, and they created an atmosphere in which we were allowed to make mistakes and learn from them. I felt as if I had landed in a huge supportive family, with every member pulling for me, an experience I guess I'd heard about but never really thought existed in the real world.

Six months into the job, I was offered the opportunity to work a few hours a week on the floor. After another six months, I was on the floor full-time. Pope's was on College Avenue, so the clientele were people who cared about their appearance and weren't put off by the spendy price tag. That meant I was exposed to a world of affluence and accomplishment that I hadn't known before. I met doctors, lawyers, UC Berkeley professors, artists, politicians, computer wonks, writers, privileged college kids, and comfortable housewives. I remember one mother lamenting her daughter's concern that she was the only kid on the playground whose house didn't have an elevator. Part of my job, though, was to make every customer feel welcomed in the salon, so I couldn't afford to affect an attitude about anyone. Flexibility and diplomacy were built into the profession, qualities I filed away in the off chance that I might one day meet my father and half siblings. I had no idea who they were or what they were like, so I'd have to be ready for anything.

Occasionally, customers would ask about my education and if I was planning to be a hairdresser for the rest of my life. I'd tell them that I went to El Cerrito High School, but I would omit the part about being a dropout. The whole subject of my family and education was an embarrassment to me, so the less I said about it, the better. But it gnawed at me, being a dropout.

I started thinking more and more about my discarded education, and as soon as I decided I wanted to try for a diploma, I went right to Mr. B. I knew it must have killed him when I turned my back on high school, but he never gave up on me and always left the door open to my coming back. Sure enough, I didn't have to ask twice. When I was ready, he pulled some strings and got me into an adult education program. In June of 1980, a month before my twentieth birthday, I received my high school diploma from Albany Adult School.

M y professional life was proceeding apace, but my love life
was getting off to a rockier start. If it's true what they say
about women dating and then marrying men like their fathers,
I was certainly starting out with a handicap, given the two
male role models in my life: one an alcoholic abuser and the
other an impossibly idealized fantasy. I wasn't aware that I was
attracted to a type, but looking back, I see that I was looking
for someone who kind of embodied both these father figures.
He had to be a badass but not a bully: someone who could protect me and would fall so head over heels in love with me that
he would never leave. You know, a James Dean type, someone
who had my stepfather's toughness but who could channel his
macho for good.

A few months before graduating from Adult Ed, I fell for
Aaron. Susan and I were throwing a party, and Aaron arrived
with a group of girls, one who knew Susan's boyfriend.

I was overdue for a boyfriend. Four years before, I had had
a one-night stand with a nineteen-year-old. It was a night
of sixteen-ounce cans of Pabst Blue Ribbon, a record player
spinning the Gregg Allman *Laid Back* album in repeat mode,
and candlelight flickering from a wax-dripped Chianti bottle.
(Judging by the multicolored wax buildup, that night was not
its first tour of duty.) The next morning, I left without my vir-
ginity, and I never saw or heard from that guy again. During
the next few years, I may have wanted more than a hit-and-
run affair, but my unpredictable home life caused me to think
twice. There were no attractions strong enough to expose a
boy to my alcoholic mother and stepfather.

But now that I was on my own, I liked Aaron right away.

He had his own car—a Chevrolet Chevelle—and the sexy swagger to go with it. Before he left the party, I gave him my phone number, and the next day he used it.

Finally, I felt wanted. Having Aaron's arm around my shoulders gave me a sense of belonging, and I fell in love with that feeling. Every time he called or came by, I'd light up like a solar flare in the dark cosmos. The only problem was that every time he left, I was afraid he'd disappear and lose interest in seeing me again. Our time together was exhilarating, but the time apart was excruciating. It didn't take long before I found myself chasing one feeling as fast as I was running from the other.

My insecurity felt deep-rooted and shameful, so of course I tried to hide it. Without any real language to articulate vulnerability, I positioned myself behind a take-it-or-leave-it facade. Beneath it, though, I was desperately pursuing a one-sided quest: I believed that *I* had to perform for my keep, but I had no particular expectations that Aaron do the same. So I gave affection, adoration, and support without question but didn't expect him to jump through any particular hoops on my behalf.

I even went so far as to choose him over my friend Susan. The duplex Susan and I shared was proving to be too small for her and me and our unofficial roommates—the boyfriends— so when things got tense and a decision had to be made, I picked my boyfriend over my girlfriend. It wasn't because he loved me more or was a better friend; it's that it was easier for me to say goodbye to her than to set limits with him. I allowed Aaron to come and go in my life as he pleased, and I refused to consider how that might impact my best friend.

Susan and I remained friends, but the relationship lost its comfortable slouch. We didn't see each other as often, and when we did, it was in larger social settings—parties and nightclubs—that didn't allow for in-depth conversations or meaningful connection. I realize now that I reacted to this "breakup" the same way I dealt with my insecurity around Aaron: I kept my feelings hidden and acted like it was no big deal. And it was that blithe dismissal, the I-don't-care of it, that probably doomed our friendship more than the actual physical separation. Clearly, one of many lessons I needed to learn was about how to communicate more openly, not to mention, how not to be one of those girls who ditches her friends the minute she finds a boyfriend. But that kind of maturity was beyond me at the time. Besides, another issue was beginning to gnaw at me once again: my absent father.

I moved into a tiny studio apartment on Solano Avenue, and that's where I began the search for my absent father. There were so many unanswered questions, starting with the peculiar variant of Mr. Abbott's name on my birth certificate: Gerrick Abbott Ellis.

I had always assumed that Gerrick Abbott was my father, mainly because of those rapturous comments my mother used to make about him. So why was Ellis attached to his name on a legal document? My mother had been married to Eugene Ellis, but she had filed for divorce four years before I was born. Still, I didn't want to rule out any possibilities. Maybe my mother had had some impulsive romantic reunion with Mr. Ellis years after their marriage ended, and maybe Mr. Abbott, the adored-but-married lover, simply stepped in to help. Pregnancy with one's ex-husband might raise eyebrows, but crazier things do happen.

Yet another possibility was that there had been some altogether unknown man that my mother was hiding for some reason. Repugnant as the idea was, I had braced myself for the possibility that my conception could have been the result of an assault, a nonconsensual attack, the pain of which kept my mother zipped up tight, unable or unwilling to discuss it. I just didn't know.

I also had no idea what kind of agreements had been made, if any, between my father and my mother about any potential relationship with me. I didn't know whether the door to him was shut and bolted or if there was a chance that a father/daughter relationship was out there waiting for me. Even if a bond with my biological father was *not* in the cards,

I wanted him to know that I existed. I also wanted to find out what kind of person had supplied my X chromosome and contributed to my DNA.

I needed to start somewhere, so I identified Mr. Abbott as my most likely candidate. Either he was or wasn't my father, and I had to set the record straight.

I returned to my mother's strongbox. A couple of years had passed since I first glanced at the contents, and this time I was prepared to look more closely. I found the two letters marked "Ellis vs. Abbott" between the attorneys discussing "child support," but they didn't identify what child they were referring to, so they weren't much help. Then I found a note that my mother had written to Mr. Abbott when his monthly check failed to arrive. I studied the message she had jotted on a small slip of paper. It read:

Dear Gerrick,
Is there some reason why I didn't receive the $90.00 check for child support for October 1975.

It was inside an envelope that had been marked by the post office, "Return to sender." I knew my mother's flinty temper, so I thought her note was less a question than a demand. Ending her sentence with a period, not a question mark, was likely intentional. She really wasn't asking for any of his excuses; she was pointing out his failure. She was on it, no question mark needed.

I continued leafing through the papers, looking for anything with Mr. Abbott's name on it, and found a half sheet of heavy, embossed paper that almost looked like a diploma but turned out to be Sean's birth certificate. It was far more ornate than my certificate, with a raised golden crest, an artist's rendition of the hospital, and a vivid red band printed on the paper. The text was in ornate calligraphy except for the particulars regarding my brother, which were typed in. He and my mother both have the last name Ellis on the document, but under the heading "Family History," his father's full name is listed as "Gerrick Dean Ellis." Dean? *That* was a name I'd never heard before. Perhaps it was a clue, so I filed it away in the back of my mind.

I went through all of the other documents in the strongbox but didn't find anything else with any configurations of the names Eugene, Gerrick, Ellis, Abbott, or Dean. With many patrilineal possibilities to consider, I was also starting to feel a bit anxious about whether I even had the right to pursue them. Searching for a man who probably wanted his identity left unknown made me feel like a stalker, a gate-crasher. I also felt a disapproving glare coming from my mother's grave. If she had wanted me to know who my father was, she would have made damn sure I did.

But I decided I just had to be selfish, intimidating as that felt. Nobody was giving me permission to probe, but nobody was stopping me either. For better or worse, I was ready to face whatever turned up. Besides, I was desperate to be wrong about my father's wishes in the matter. Maybe his absence had not been of his own making, and he wanted to know me as much as I wanted to know him.

I heard about the ALMA Society from one of my regular hair-dressing clients. She told me it was a nonprofit organization, founded in 1971, that maintains a database of mostly parents and their abdicated offspring. The first A in ALMA stands for "Adoptees'"—Adoptees' Liberty Movement Association—and its primary focus and advocacy is for the rights of adopted children, a distinction that I did not have. But I figured this was a community of folks who would understand my deep-rooted desire to find my missing in action father, regardless.

ALMA was not well known, and back then, their registry was more like a paper-based catalog than a computerized algorithm. The odds of a matchup between my father and me were slim, but slim was still better than none. I attended one of their local affiliate meetings in Berkeley, and after a presentation of current ALMA affairs—the telling of success stories, recommendations for search strategies, and questions and answers from the floor—I signed up to be a card-carrying member.

The facilitators at the meeting made it clear that they were not investigators or mediators. All they could do was point me in the direction of public records where I might start digging: census records, military service records, ship manifests, criminal records, voter records, and so on. That came as a real disappointment. I had fantasized about a Hollywood reversal-of-fortune movie, in which I was the lost child denied her rightful place in society, and one day I would get a call from a guardian angel saying, "I found your father, and he wants to meet you!" Alas, no such luck; the hunt was mine.

I can't say that I was on fire to pore through volumes of old records. I imagined mountains of information buried in massive folios with dizzying lines of miniscule text in swirling, cursive script. Besides not having confidence in my ability to read, period, I was afraid I wouldn't be able to decode the quill strokes from decades past. The idea of requesting access to governmental records also drained me of my most ardent intentions. How would I write that initial letter? I couldn't compose my thoughts clearly enough to state them on paper. Write? Write what? Write how? I didn't have a typewriter; my penmanship was terrible and my punctuation worse, and my spelling was atrocious. I was stuck.

I gave up on the whole idea, but it always had a way of resurfacing. And when it did, it would fill my entire being with a deep longing and a torrent of what-ifs. What if he's dead? What if he's an alcoholic? What if he's mean? What if he's wonderful but wants nothing to do with his bastard daughter? My heart wanted love and my head wanted answers, and the two profound urges kept me awake at night.

I decided that writing inquiry letters to governmental agencies and records bureaus was out of the question. But I *could* initiate a search by driving my newly purchased used sports car, a little white Volvo P1800, to downtown Oakland and pay a visit to the Alameda County Registrar of Voters Office. Even though I didn't have a current address for Gerrick Abbott, I had an old one, so that would be my first step.

The Alameda County Courthouse is a monolith that looks as if it had been lifted from the National Mall in Washington, DC. Inside, the lobby was cool and imposing, a hub lined with marble floor and walls, etched glass, and art deco–inspired ornamentation. Inside the registrar's office, I told the clerk that I was looking for voting information on the name Gerrick Abbott. I was given a microfiche reel and directed to a viewing station.

I loaded the machine and began to scroll up, down, right, and left until I came to the name Gerrick D. Abbott. That "D" popped off the screen at me; it might have stood for Dean. His address was different from the Dublin, California, address I had written down before leaving my studio, but my pulse quickened when I saw that he was born in Illinois, just like my mother. His birth year was 1931, making him just two years older than my mother—the right age. All this information had been entered on May 8, 1976, and Gerrick D. was registered as a Democrat, which meant he would have been able to vote for Jimmy Carter against Gerald Ford in the June primary. I liked that. I had done volunteer work in a Jimmy Carter campaign office while I was in high school. My mother had been unable to locate Mr. Abbott once his monthly checks stopped, but I was almost certain I just had.

But there was something else, and I could hardly hold my pencil to write it down. Right next to this Gerrick D. Abbott was a Gerry Abbott. The information on him was less complete. All it said was that he had registered to vote on August 5, 1975, and that his birthday was August 5. It didn't give his birth year. Hmmm . . . that's weird, I thought. He had registered on his birthday. Was it a coincidence? Or had it been an important event, a rite of passage, on his eighteenth birthday? If that were the case, then he would have been two months younger than my brother Sean. If this Gerry Abbott was Gerrick D. Abbott's son, that would mean the man who had been making child support payments to my mother for Sean had both a wife and a mistress pregnant at the same time.

I made several attempts to draft a letter to this man I thought might be my father. All but two of them ended up in my garbage can. Of those, I kept one and sent the other to my newly found addressee, Gerrick D. Abbott. But I reserved a sliver of skepticism. I was afraid to get my hopes up and was also a bit worried. If this Gerrick D. wasn't my Gerrick Dean, then he would be in possession of my contact information and my sensitive subject matter. I don't know exactly what I thought he'd do with it, or how he could use it against me, but it just felt strange.

I didn't tell Aaron, Susan, or anyone else what I was up to—not even my brother. Letting Sean in on my plan would require that I have a plan, and I really didn't. I wanted to meet the man, that I was sure of, but I wasn't ready for all that might entail: the emotional upheaval, the possible recriminations, or even just the awkwardness of suddenly having this new person in my life who didn't know me but might feel that he had some authority over me. It just didn't seem appropriate to subject my brother to my embryonic speculations. Plus, in an effort to assist me, he might want to take over, and I was concerned about getting lost in the process. I was also afraid that if my brother didn't approve of my actions, I might buckle, and I was already too close to that side as it was.

But hanging out so far on a limb by myself felt truly unnerving. I felt like I was begging for recognition, groveling at the feet of a laughing crowd of people who all knew who their fathers were. My thoughts were merciless. "Ha, ha, ha, look at that stupid girl, she doesn't know who she is, ha, ha, ha," is what I thought people would think and say, snickering, mocking, and shaming me. It took tremendous fortitude—or foolishness, I wasn't sure which—to rebuff those taunting thoughts.

I plowed on and composed my letter. The draft I saved is a telling snapshot of who I was back then. I tried to hold my head up. I tried to sound mature. And because I didn't know who would end up reading it, I played it safe and didn't reveal too much about myself. It's full of spelling and punctuation errors, and although I did my best to control my hand, the writing itself is shaky.

I wrote:

Dear Gerrick Abbott

Well this is by far the most difficult letter I have ever tried to write.

My name is Terry Sue and my mothers maiden name is Margaret Jean Bierman.

By now I imagine your sitting down and can see why this letter is so difficult to word.

I'm writing because I'm very curious about what you look like and who you are and I would like you to know me and what I look like.

I think I know the circumstances surrounding my mothers and your relationship and I want to assure you that my curiosity is innocent and I don't want to disrupt your family.

I have absolutly no idea what you might be thinking right now but I'm full of anticipation and hope that you will write or call soon.

Thank you

I signed off with my name, address, and phone number. I didn't mention my mother's death; I could get into that after we made contact.

I sealed and addressed the letter, and when I was at the post office, I had to force myself to release it into the mailbox. I knew that once it was literally out of my hands, it would be out of my control. All I could do was wait. Three days passed. Four days passed. A week went by and then a month.

Dejected and ashamed for trying, I had to pick myself up and dust off what little pride I had. Nobody knew how flat on my face I had fallen, nobody but the recipient of my letter and me. After a few months of silence from Mr. Abbott's end, I gave up all illusions of a surprise call. Either Mr. Abbott didn't get my letter, or he did get it and decided not to respond for any number of reasons I could only guess at. At that point, I had done all I could.

While my adventure in Fatherlandia had been a flop, I tried not to let it get me down. I didn't know if I had been completely rejected or if Mr. Abbott hadn't even set eyes on my dopey I'd-like-to-meet-you letter. It hadn't occurred to me to send the letter certified mail, so anything could have happened to it once it left my hands. In fact, I convinced myself that his wife had opened it and discarded it immediately—so it was all her fault. And because I still felt embarrassed about putting my heart on my sleeve like that, I was relieved to turn my attention elsewhere as quickly as I could.

In many ways, this was the point in my life when the downhill trajectory of my childhood made a definitive U-turn. My scramble from poverty and illegitimacy was fading to a distasteful memory as I was entering the middle of the middle class and enjoying many of its trappings. I was becoming a successful hairdresser. I no longer had to wear secondhand clothing—unless I wanted to. I could go to doctors of my choice. I washed my face with pricey cleansers, attended avant-garde theater productions, and sipped wine while nibbling Brie and baguette at art gallery openings.

I didn't have much to complain about, but my chase for the good life also had a slightly manic quality that reflected the power of what I was running *from*. I was over twenty-one and had cash to burn and friends to burn it with. So I put on heavier makeup, hung out in trendier clubs, ate at fancier restaurants, and sniffed my first line of cocaine. It's also when I started drinking more than ever before.

Until that point, I had been a cautious drinker, imbibing as a way of blending in with my friends. I was too much of a control freak to allow myself to get totally hammered. Drunken antics reminded me too much of my parents, and I didn't want any part of that unpredictable behavior. Fortunately, I had a high tolerance and could drink a fair amount before it showed.

Once I discovered amphetamines, I found that I could consume way more alcohol, and with that, my appetite for it only intensified. I didn't drink in the morning, and I didn't drink alone, but I drank whenever I wanted, and I started to want it almost every day of the week. Liquor just seemed to bathe any occasion in a feeling of gaiety and good will, and fill me with personality and courage. But it didn't take long before that fearlessness turned into recklessness. I drove while intoxicated. I spent money that I had intended to save. I missed work because of being hungover. I even began to avoid my straighter friends and became chummy with a few shady characters. But still, my party life looked nothing like the life I had grown up in, so the idea of addiction couldn't have been further from my mind. Intoxication was just part of living the high life.

My love life, however, I *knew* was on the skids. Aaron and I broke up and got back together over and over, and during one of the separations, I had a brief fling with a married man. He was a charismatic punk rocker, and we hooked up the day he returned from his honeymoon. Classy, eh? Sex, drugs, and rock and roll, baby: fidelity and trust were from another kind of playbook. I spent an enormous amount of mental space plotting and planning, fretting and fantasizing about what I would say and how I would say it to these guys.

Nevertheless, there was one unambiguously positive turn of events amidst these ups and downs; I read my first book. Until that time, I was pretty much in denial about the fact that I didn't know how to read, which resulted in my total indifference to the written word. But then, there was a particular incident that set my big shift into motion.

I was cutting a fellow's hair, a guy who had become a regular of mine, Robert. He was a total computer geek: fastidious in his appearance, with commercially laundered shirts and slacks and a breast-pocket protector where a ballpoint pen was always at the ready. And because he had heard that his idol, Bill Gates, got haircuts every three weeks, he did the same. He was an odd duck, but I found his quirkiness appealing.

One day we were talking about something, I don't remember what, but he used the word "pathology." I didn't know what it meant, and when I asked him, he was incredulous. Our exchange went something like:

"You don't know what 'pathology' means?"

"No."

"It means the study of illness."

"Oh."

That was the moment when my inability to read felt like a crisis that needed addressing.

Robert may not have been judging me, but I was judging myself. I knew I wasn't stupid, but I also knew that not being able to fully grasp the written word was holding me back. There had been so many occasions when I had only pretended to understand what was being said to me. Now, seemingly overnight, I aspired to feeling at ease in the company of better-educated folks. Even more, I wanted to feel intellectually confident *myself*.

It also weighed on me that I had done such a poor job on the letter I sent to Mr. Abbott. If I were ever to attempt another one, I would have to do better. And I had little doubt that if I could become a better reader, I could become a better writer. Perhaps if I made myself shine with a little finer polish, the man would give me the time of day.

I decided I needed to teach myself how to read, one word at a time, so I drove to the El Cerrito public library to check out a book. I promised myself I would read it cover to cover, not pretend and not cheat. I was going to read every single word and not move on to the next sentence until I was certain that I had understood the one I'd just finished. I had no preferences when it came to literary genres; mystery, science fiction, romance were all the same to me. I just wanted the book to be big.

I selected *My Many Years*, a newly released *six-hundred-page* autobiography by Arthur Rubinstein, a classical pianist I had never heard of. I was just as nervous applying for a library card as I had been when I applied for my driver's license. Full of insecurities, I found even the friendly librarian intimidating. My fear was that I would be told I had to pass a reading proficiency exam before I could get the card. A part of me understood that such thinking was nonsense, but I was habitually afraid of being judged and found lacking; wanting a library card just played right into that. It was a tiny victory when the librarian handed over the card and book.

At home, I didn't talk to a soul about my self-imposed challenge. I wasn't sure I would succeed, and I didn't want anyone to interrogate me on my progress. Also, I needed total silence in order to concentrate, and I didn't want anyone around when I was trying to focus.

The first sentence on the dust jacket of *My Many Years* showed me how tough this was going to be. It read, "With the same charm, candor, total recall, and brilliance as a raconteur that made *My Young Years* (his first twenty-nine) a best-selling delight, the great pianist Arthur Rubinstein now regales

us with a lavish account of the sixty-four years since." I didn't
know what "regales" and "raconteur" meant, so the dictionary
quickly became my friend. But it didn't help me with the second sentence. That one had the phrase "haut monde" in it. I
was familiar with the phrase "haute cuisine" as a way of referring to fancy food, but "haut monde" was new to me. I looked
in the H section of the dictionary and then the M section, but
it wasn't there. I decided that the sentence had something to
do with Arthur Rubinstein making a splash with the people
of South America, so I read on.

Fortunately, Rubinstein's writing was easier to follow than
the publisher's jacket synopsis, but it still caused me trouble.
Initially, I had the hardest time transitioning from one line of
text to the next. I struggled to train my eye to find the next
row of words as I moved across the page from left to right and
back to the left side again. Bookmarks helped, but not always.
Some of the time I would use one to cover the parts I had yet
to read, and other times I would cover the parts I'd already
finished. Either way, above or below, I found the surrounding
text to be a distraction. I tried cutting a slot into a solid piece
of paper to reveal only the line of text I was working on, but
sometimes I'd lose track if I moved the opening down too far.
It was slow going, but I had the power of my conviction to
drive me on, and the plot was developing in my imagination.

His story fascinated me. In addition to his career as a
renowned classical pianist, Rubinstein's life was full of inter-
national travel, personal experiences during the Hitler reign,
love, glamour, and celebrity. His storytelling was dignified
and restrained but also warm and inviting. It was as if I had sat
down with a new friend who proceeded to tell me all about his
exciting adventures. With a mug of coffee or a glass of wine
at my side, I stuck to my plan of not moving on to the next

sentence until I was sure I understood the one I'd finished.

It took several months to finish that book, but I was thrilled with my accomplishment and decided to keep going. After *My Many Years* I read another whopper, Marion Zimmer Bradley's *The Mists of Avalon* (though this one clocked in at just under four hundred pages). And there were others: *The Deptford Trilogy* by Robertson Davies, *One Hundred Years of Solitude* by Gabriel García Márquez, Anne Rice's *Interview with the Vampire*, and *Education of Oversoul Seven*, a trippy perception-bending novel by Jane Roberts, to name a few.

But as my reading confidence was improving, I suffered another stinging embarrassment. I was at a party when a group started talking about the Dalai Lama and the people of Tibet. One of the girls asked me if I knew where Tibet was, and I guessed Canada. That answer was met with howling laughter. Yes, it was humiliating, but their mocking jolted me into doing something more about my education. The books I was enjoying, the customers I wanted to talk with, and the shame I was feeling about my lack of schooling all led to my taking another step up the education ladder. I began remedial English classes at the junior college. Those soon led to general education courses, and after almost nine years of that, I was inspired to apply to Mills College. And I was accepted!

Before signing up for my very first English class, I had purchased a new kind of electric typewriter: a twenty-pound, portable word processor. That fancy machine is what made writing possible for me. I detested the sight of my own handwriting, but now I could hand in homework that was at least legible. The processor also had a spelling and punctuation checker that fed me hints when I was on the wrong track. For the first time, I was learning to read and write like an adult.

The courses I took challenged me to develop another

skill that had been neglected until then: critical thinking. It was all I could do to read the course material, but then I had to identify themes, analyze topic sentences and conclusions, understand the difference between a metaphor and a symbol, and learn to spot things like foreshadowing and analogies. I was introduced to concepts such as moral ambiguity, irony, absurdity, and existentialism, all of which were new to me.

My first papers were a mess. I found the professor's red ink so humiliating that I didn't even wait to get home to throw away my returned assignments: they went right in the campus garbage cans. At that point, it just wasn't in me to scrutinize what I had done right and what I had done wrong. All I saw were the mistakes—proof that I didn't know what I was doing and that I didn't belong.

Bruising as that was, I didn't quit. I knew I had something to prove to myself—that I wasn't an ignorant fool, and that I was someone who mattered. By all outward appearances, I was confident and secure and had loads of friends. But beneath the surface, I felt alone and afraid of being abandoned. Of all the people I admired, the ones I respected the most were those who weren't afraid to show their hand in the world. I looked up to people who didn't hide, who held their heads up and were confident about expressing who they were or what they thought. I wasn't one of those types, but I wanted to be, and the ability to think critically and articulate a point of view seemed essential to making that transition.

Eventually I started to get the hang of it; I even got so that I was getting Bs and As on much of my work. And the more I branched out, the more history, science, philosophy, and mathematics I studied, the stronger my powers of observation and discernment became. I also came to see that what I felt about my particular circumstances in life was not unique, and certainly not shameful or bizarre. Questions of who we are, where we come from, and why it all matters have been asked throughout the ages, so I wasn't wrong to seek answers to these essential questions in my *own* life. The confidence I was gaining on all these fronts allowed me take a more dispassionate and investigative attitude toward my past—one that would have served me well in my search for my father, if only I hadn't been derailed by another personal upheaval.

Aaron and I broke up for the last time, and in a way that focused my emotional life in a completely different direction. Before, when we separated, I felt so desperate—like a junkie in need of a fix—that all I wanted was to get back together, no questions asked. So we would never talk about why the rift had occurred; I just took him back and felt immense relief. But this time forgiveness wasn't possible.

One day, Aaron came home with a hickey on his neck, and it wasn't from me; it turned out it was from Susan, my friend and onetime roommate. She and Aaron had gone to a club the night before, but since I had to work the next day, I had stayed home. When I saw the mark on his neck, I accused him of getting it from her, hoping that he would flatly reject such a suggestion. But he didn't.

The two of them needed to tell me what was going on, but neither one could say the words, so I guess this was their way of showing me. I knew right then the jig was up for Aaron and me. He had cheated before but never with one of my close friends. This was different, and we both knew it. The next day I told him he needed to be out by the time I got back, and he was. He moved in with Susan, and they've been together ever since.

At first, it was a roaring hell, as despair and fury slammed into me with equal force. I was so aggrieved that I wanted to strip their skin and douse them both with salt. I felt cast out, deserted, and wholly disregarded—made all the worse, I'm sure, because it called up all the same feelings I had had in my family. First it was my mother, my father, and my step-father who had abandoned me; now it was my boyfriend and my, at one time, best friend. I just could not make peace with any of it.

For my own preservation, I eventually resorted to the survival tactic that had spared me in the past: denial. I sent my thoughts elsewhere, and one of the places they went was Europe.

The dollar was strong, and it appeared as though every other person I came across was either going to or had just returned from there. So I decided to take four weeks and visit England, France, Spain, and Italy.

My list of activities and sights to see kept me busy and excited everyday. I spent hours in museums, cathedrals, and cafés. I shopped for the trendiest clothes. I became adept at converting dollars into pounds, francs, and lira. In Paris, I learned to worship at the altar of Pernod, an anise-flavored liquor designed in the 1920s to replace absinthe. I didn't make any friends while traveling, but all in all, it was a great, if temporary, antidote to the pain I was feeling before I left.

When I got home, I was able to slip comfortably back into school and work, but I was still wrapped pretty tight. When I was alone with my thoughts, I'd unravel. When no one was looking, I found myself crying for no apparent reason. And my alcohol consumption was escalating . . . fast. I was drinking every day, and heavily every weekend. Alone or with friends, it didn't matter. I kept beer, wine, gin, tonic, limes, and green olives on hand at all times, and I took pride in owning the appropriate glass and stemware for each variety of liquor I consumed. Champagne flutes, martini glasses, and sake cups were in the cupboard alongside shot glasses and wine goblets. Every holiday had an associated beverage: Valentine's Day was champagne, Cinco de Mayo was tequila, Christmas was brandy and eggnog, and on it went. If it wasn't a holiday, it was "I need a drink because it's Monday." Tuesdays and Thursdays were typically uneventful, so I drank to spice them up. Wednesday was worth toasting because it was halfway to the weekend. And Friday, the weekend was finally here!

Saturdays were the big prize since I didn't have to go to work the next day. That's when I'd shrug off whatever limited restraint I had practiced and drink to my heart's content. Then, to counteract some of the effect of the alcohol, I would use cocaine to stay upright. And once both those substances were in my system, cigarettes seemed like a satisfying addition, and I could go through a couple of packs in a weekend.

My attitude toward it all, however, hadn't changed from before. I still convinced myself that my drinking was different enough from what I had seen as a kid that I didn't have a real problem. After all, I never blacked out or forgot my actions. I never ended up in strange places with strange people. I didn't crash cars or go to jail, and I had a sizable group of friends who drank just like I did. Alcoholism was something *other* people struggled with. But there's no denying that I was headed for a crash—maybe not sooner, but it was coming.

If anyone had asked, I would have said everything in my life at that point was fine. I was having way too much fun drinking, dancing, working, and hanging out with friends for anyone to suspect any different. But there was a shadow side to all that frivolity that finally showed up one morning after a night of bingeing. I had put myself to bed but was too sprung to get my eyes to close. My ears were ringing, and my heart fluttered like a trapped bird. I wasn't asleep and I wasn't dreaming, but I had the sense of being inside the longest, darkest tunnel, with a pinprick of light at the end that I understood to represent death. For only a flash, I considered letting go and allowing its gravitational pull to suck me in. I thought, if I die right here, my friends would be sad, but no one would really care if I were alive or not. I thought I was on the verge of a heart attack, but rather than succumbing to it, I pulled myself together with a shower and a few forced bites of food.

The episode sure scared me, but it wasn't enough to scare me straight. Instead, I blamed that night's particular combination of chemicals: it wasn't me; it was the mezcal, cocaine, marijuana, and packs of cigarettes. Still, I decided to slow down a bit and make an effort to reconnect with a few of my more stable friends. One of them introduced me to an eligible bachelor, Lyle Dumont, and I was off to the love-will-fix-me races once again. Somewhere in the bowels of my thinking, I figured that my inchoate fears of being unwanted and unlovable would be assuaged by a new romance.

Lyle Dumont was by far the most educated and quick-witted fellow I had ever met. He lived in Los Angeles, wore a suit and tie to work, and earned well into a six-figure income running a municipal airport. We struck up a long-distance love affair. He was kind and generous, and surprisingly gregarious for a bookworm. He had a large social circle and mingled well with all of my friends. Together we'd gad about, going to parties, cafés, rare and used bookstores, art galleries, dance halls, supper clubs, and dimly lit bars. We were also alike in our drinking styles: hard liquor, and lots of it.

We started out strong. I even thought he might be "the one." After about three or four months, we started talking about living together, although not a word had been spoken about marriage. I took it as a given that I would be the one to move. Perhaps that should have been the first sign that something was amiss. But I told myself it was no big deal—his white collar was more important than my pink smock—and I arranged to move to Southern California. But just as it had been with Aaron, I was too insecure to pay attention to my nagging doubts and say, "I think this might be a mistake." Plus, by the time I was getting cold feet, I had given notice at work, and my friends had thrown me a going-away party. It felt too late to turn back.

It didn't take long for my doubts to sound off. As we drove along the spine of California, down desolate (at the time) Highway 5, it was the peal of alarm—not wedding bells—I heard. I had put my own identity on the back burner to make this move, and Lyle's presence did nothing to prevent me from feeling bad about it. I chalked the clangor in my head up to fatigue, certain it would go away with a few good nights' rest.

But it didn't. Instead of flying back and forth for our jet-set weekends, we were suddenly stuck with each other—every single day. And it was a hard landing. Out of my element, I felt like dead weight. I perked up as best I could when he'd come home from work, but my pep was a total put-on. I didn't want to be found out that I had made such a colossal mistake, so I prettied up my face and the house and did what I could to appear pleased with our domestic arrangement.

But it became clear that Lyle and I didn't really know each other—certainly not well enough for me to have uprooted my whole life for him. I knew he made a ton of money, but I didn't know a thing about how he managed it beyond what we spent together. We never talked about our income disparity, or who was expected to pay for what. I had never seen him angry, and he had never seen me sad. I was so giddy with the excitement of moving to a new land, starting a new life, and laying a path to marriage that I gave almost no thought to how I was upending what little foundation I had been creating for myself in El Cerrito.

Meanwhile, as I carried on my charade, things continued to go downhill. Professionally, I was a total flop. Without an established clientele, I couldn't get any salon owners to talk to me. I had gone from being a big fish in a small pond to being invisible inside a sea of beauty shops. Time passed without my earning a cent. Lyle and I continued our flitting about town, spending money like we always had, but now we were doing it several days a week as opposed to a couple of times a month. I didn't want to be seen as stingy or needy, so I insisted on paying my own way, and sometimes I picked up the tab for both of us. Pretending to be financially secure, I spent large sums on food, drink, new clothes, and the biggest drain, cocaine. I also discovered that speed, otherwise known as poor man's cocaine, was stronger and lasted longer, so I added that to my repertoire. The amphetamines allowed me to drink greater quantities of alcohol without getting ugly. Needless to say, I blew through money like a Santa Ana wind during Indian summer.

Oh, and I also convinced myself that Lyle had the hots for the next-door neighbor. On day one, while Lyle and I were unpacking the U-Haul, she called with a supposed emergency. He gave me a peck on the cheek and said he'd be right back. The box of dishes I was holding suddenly made me sick with regret. When he returned, he wheeled a Vespa scooter into the middle of the kitchen. Apparently, she had stolen it, and he agreed to hide it for her. Wanting to be a good sport, I went along, but I felt like she was letting me know that I was not the only chick moving into Lyle Dumont's house. Nothing ever really happened between them (as far as I know), but it was just another antagonism that fed my misgivings.

Instinctively, I sensed disaster, but I couldn't behave in a way that might have prevented it. In my gut I felt disrespected, but worse than that, I felt deserving of such low regard. I was too proud to speak up and too insecure to act decisively on my own behalf. When his friends came over and wouldn't leave for days, I said nothing. When his cats sprayed on my clothes, I laughed it off as a petty annoyance. When he spoke long distance to his parents and made no mention of me, I pretended not to notice. But all this effort to blend in just had the opposite effect. I ended up disappearing, and Lyle began to fade away as well. I couldn't really blame him, but at the same time, he could have been a little more observant. I'm a good actor, but I'm not that good; he could have noticed I was tanking.

The whole thing blew up on the morning of January 28, 1986. That was the day the space shuttle *Challenger* launched into orbit. I still hadn't found a job, and after Lyle would go to work in the morning, I'd pull the curtains closed and hang out in my bathrobe. An hour before his return, I'd shower and dress. That fateful morning, I watched the news on TV as I lay in bed, with a drink by my side. I was consistently drinking by myself in the morning during that period: coffee with brandy, vodka and orange juice, vodka and tomato juice, beer, Kahlúa and cream—whatever was cold, and whatever was around. Both hungover and intoxicated, I was immersed in self-absorbed dissatisfaction.

I gazed at the television as the rocket cleared the tower and began to pick up speed. It was all proceeding as planned until the explosion occurred a little more than a minute later. If it had been any other institution, I would have assumed sure death, but this was NASA, so I held out hope that the seven astronauts would somehow parachute back to Earth, would somehow come out alive. And when it became obvious that they wouldn't, I was thunderstruck.

I was devastated that these heroes had been incinerated, and I couldn't help but think of the old cliché "Life is too short." Somehow, at that moment, the whole tragic event shook me out of my incapacitating self-pity. Life *was* too short, so I got on the phone to see if I could reclaim the good parts of what I had so blithely waltzed away from in the Bay Area. I called my old bosses to see if I could have my job back, and they assured me that I could. I called a friend and asked if she knew anyone who would rent me a room for a while. She said her mother might. "After all, my mom is famous for taking in stray cats," was her comment to me. It was a joke, but it fit, so I didn't take offense.

When I told Lyle I was going back home, he didn't protest. I guess we both just knew we had come to the end, so there was no point in rehashing all the sorry details. It was all very anticlimactic, but better that than an ugly blowup, I guess. At any rate, I was gone within the week.

My friend's mother, Helen, had agreed to take me in,

temporarily—and it turned out to be a great move for me. Her home was a Craftsman in the foothills of Oakland. Its attractive interior was anchored by richly oiled woodwork. My room was upstairs. The bed in that guest room was made up with a white-eyeleted down comforter and layers of lacy sham-covered pillows; the walls were painted baby blue, the furnishings Victorian, and it was all crisp, clean, and neat as a pin.

I couldn't help but compare Helen's lifestyle to mine. Her home was spotless from top to bottom, no cobwebs at the ceiling and no dust on the baseboards. Decorative vases filled with fragrant bouquets adorned many of the rooms, and sunlight streamed in through streakless windows. Not only that, it was a drama-free zone. As lady of the house, Helen went about her day with well-paced purpose; her movements were calm, her actions thoughtful, and her activities were planned and executed with a high degree of predictability.

I, of course, was pretty much the opposite—and it was after a night of drinking and drugging that I finally took stock of just how much that needed to change. It was my practice to enter Helen's house by way of the kitchen door, and on that morning, Helen was at her stove preparing the morning tea. She was in her pastel chenille bathrobe, and I was still in my trendy black. I knew I reeked of cigarettes and gin. From a night of cocaine and martinis, my lipstick and mascara were smeared, my jaw clenched, and my eyes fixed open like a scared beast in the darkest forest. I scurried past her with only the briefest greeting.

I had to be at work by ten o'clock, and if I was going to make it, I had to try and get an hour of sleep, a ridiculous idea given how hopped up on amphetamines I was. In my room, I stripped and put my fetid self to bed. Thoughts raced around in my head like a pack of crazed monkeys; I felt acutely that I had defiled Helen's pristine home. That's when I had a flash of insight. It seems odd that so many years had gone by before it happened, but I suddenly understood that I was just as hooked on alcohol as my mother had been. God help me, I thought, and in the next moment I knew I had to stop drinking. That realization struck me with as much force as if I had slammed my car into a brick wall.

I had to stop not because I had been caught but because I knew that being hooked meant not being able to quit when I wanted. I had to admit that my alcohol intake could not be controlled by my determination, or peer pressure, or common sense. Morals, personality, good intentions, none of it mattered when it came to managing how much I would or would not drink. Before that morning, if I wanted another drink, I would have it, even if it meant showing up for work when I was still intoxicated from the night before. That morning, loud and clear, I got it that I had to quit drinking—not taper off but stop, 100 percent, cold turkey, for real, for good, and forever.

The thought of never drinking ever again was about as sobering as a bucket of ice water in the face. Drinking had become such a habit that I couldn't be certain that I wouldn't just accidentally pour myself something without realizing what I was doing. It was like reaching for the light switch when you know full well there's a power failure going on. What was also crystal clear on that morning was that my off switch was just as faulty as my mother's had been, and that I could no longer be contemptuous of her weakness when I had the same affliction. We were both alcoholics.

I called a childhood friend whom I had dropped when she got sober. She didn't hold my absence against me and suggested that I find an Alcoholics Anonymous meeting to go to. She also said that habits tend to be intertwined, so I should get busy making some less stressful changes, such as driving a different route to and from work so that I wouldn't go past the same old liquor stores, avoiding restaurants where liquor was served, and getting rid of all the bottle openers and drug paraphernalia in my purse. She even advised me to rearrange my furniture, just to disrupt the familiar setting where I had been comfortable drinking.

I called AA, and they told me there was a "beginner's meeting" at the end of that day. Before leaving the house, I tied a piece of string around my wrist to remind myself of the meeting—and not to drink in the meantime. At work, every mirror reflected a haggard young woman I didn't recognize: me, scared to death that I wouldn't be able to conquer my drug and alcohol habits. I thought my life was over; I would never laugh, dance, make friends, enjoy food, or have sex again. I was scheduled to go to Mexico in a few weeks with three other friends, and I thought I would need to cancel those plans because I was certain margaritas and cervezas would get the better of me.

As advised, I did make it to the AA beginner meeting, and I was spellbound by the first guy who got up to talk about his drinking history and his road to recovery. He stood in front of all those people and spoke truth like I had never heard it spoken before. I took him to be humble, sincere, and wholly believable.

When he was done, the meeting was opened up to the group, but everybody seemed to clam up. To this day, I'm amazed, and amused, by what happened next. Since nobody was saying anything, the speaker decided to call on someone. Looking back, I'm sure he was looking at someone up front when he said, "Terry, is there anything you would like to say?" I was seated farther back, but, not knowing a single person in the room, I made an audacious assumption and thought he was calling on me. So before the intended Terry spoke up, I choked out the words, "My name is Terry, and I'm an alcoholic." Dozens of heads did a hard pivot to look at who was talking.

Tearfully, I told the group that I had a string around my wrist because I was afraid I would start drinking again as soon as I wasn't so hungover. I told them that I had made several declarations to go on diets right after completing a huge meal, but as soon as I got hungry again, the diet plan would go out the window, and I was afraid the same thing would happen with my drinking.

The speaker responded by telling me, "You *will* need to find a way to eat, but you never have to drink alcohol again, one day at a time." I had already gone longer since my last drink then I had gone in years, so the strategy of taking sobriety in small manageable bits made sense to me, although I was looking at one *minute* at a time and one *hour* at a time instead of one day at a time. Honestly, every second that went by without me running out to a bar or a liquor store felt like an accomplishment. I had no idea how I was going to keep it up. How was I going to sever ties with a crutch that had become so central in my life?

When the meeting ended, several well-intentioned people came up to me, and I was horrified. Squeaky-clean men and women were introducing themselves, handing me their phone numbers, and encouraging me to call them. They gave me various pamphlets and wallet cards that had helpful sobriety tips written on them. I panicked. I was too paranoid to accept that all of those strangers could really care whether

I kicked the booze habit or not. I suspected that I was being drawn into some kind of cult. I thought they saw me as low-hanging fruit, ripe for the picking. If I let them have their way, soon they would have me going door to door soliciting for recruits, ringing a bell in airports to call for converts, turning over my bank accounts to some fearless leader.

I convinced myself that I wasn't as bad off as some of the participants I saw hanging out on the fringe, and that if I kept going to meetings, I would eventually tell myself that I *didn't* have a drinking problem. I knew how clever my brain could be. I could seize on any excuse to drink, and "I'm not *that* bad" would be an excellent rationalization. Before getting home, my infinite ego with an inferiority complex came to the conclusion that those meetings were a threat to my sobriety commitment, and I would be better off avoiding them. If I wanted to stop drinking, it would be wise to stay away from those *real* down-and-outers. I did myself no favors with that judgment. The truth of the matter was that I was terrified to face a life of total abstinence, and the room was full of people doing just that. They had a phrase, "Take what you need and leave the rest," but I took what I didn't need and left the rest.

With my jaw clenched and knuckles whitened, I actually did manage to stay sober. I moved into an apartment of my own and signed up for another community college class. I fuelled myself with sugar, caffeine, work, school, and several nights a week of going to movies instead of bars. The more days that passed that way, the more I wanted to reward my efforts with a drink—but I held firm. At night, though, I would put my head on my pillow feeling as though I had outrun a lumbering monster one more day, but I couldn't imagine how I was going to keep it up. I feared that the monster would catch up to me sooner or later, and I was doomed to die the same miserable death as my mother, too intoxicated to communicate the need for help.

I became desperate to gain a fuller understanding of who, what, or where my alcoholism had come from. So one afternoon I returned to my mother's strongbox. I didn't know what I was looking for; I just had some idea that maybe my mother's past would hold a clue to my present. This time I focused on the small collection of photo negatives that were inside two yellow Kodak Printing envelopes—one dated 8/9/47 and the other from 5/28/55—years before I was born. Combined, there were about two dozen undeveloped photos. I was afraid no lab would be equipped to handle such old negatives. The films were faded and difficult to make out. There was one place in Berkeley, however, that my photographer friends swore by, so I gave them what I had and hoped for the best.

My anticipation had grown exponentially between the time I was told that the negatives could be salvaged and the day when I finally held the photographs in my hands. These were no ordinary pictures; they were never-before-seen remnants of my mother's past, and I wondered if they might show her with my father. I paid the cashier and was handed my package. I had the sense that I might need to sit down, but there were no seats available in the print shop, so I waited until I was secure within the confines of my car before peering at each black-and-white snapshot.

What I saw was my mother as a girl and a young woman, aspects of her life I had spent little time considering. By August of 1947 she would have been almost fourteen, and in 1955 she would have been twenty-one. My mother rarely spoke about her childhood; it was one of many unhappy subjects she avoided. She was never entirely certain who her parents were because she didn't have a birth certificate. For all she knew, she might even have been adopted herself. All she ever told me was that her mother had died young and that her father traveled a lot for work. She mentioned having to live with relatives and resented being shuffled from home to home. But if she had any feelings of injustice about not knowing her birth origins or about the instability of her young life, those feelings didn't translate into a need to assure me on those same fronts.

In a couple of the newly developed pictures was a man whom I understood to be "Granddad Bierman." That's what my older brothers called him. He was my mother's father, legal or biological. With a patient and indulgent smile, he posed for the photographer, presumably my teenaged mother—his only child. He looked relaxed in his stance, leaning against a split-rail fence with most of his weight on one leg and acres of farmland behind him. Granddad Bierman's facial expression reminded me of Spencer Tracy—affable, slightly serious, but completely nonthreatening. He lived in Missouri at the end of his life and passed away before I was five. I don't know if he ever laid eyes on me, but I don't think so.

Several of my mother's pictures showed her with a girl about her same age. I remembered that my mother had one friend she exchanged annual Christmas cards with, and I wondered if the girl was that friend. Her name was Shirley Stanton, and she lived in Decatur, Illinois. A couple of the shots had two slightly older boys in them, sweethearts judging by the way they were hanging on the girls. One of them was quite the acrobat; he's doing handstands in two of the pictures. My mother is seated next to the trickster, wearing a short-sleeved blouse that is buttoned to her neck and a high-waisted dark skirt that covers her knees. Her hands rest in her lap, and her sandaled feet are demurely crossed at her ankles. All four of the young people were fit and well groomed.

Then there are the pictures from 1955, five years after she was married to Eugene Ellis and one year before she divorced him. Eugene looked nothing like the two boys in the 1947 pictures. For one thing, his shirt was off and his chest appeared to be hairless and flabby. The hair on his head was uncombed—spiky before spiked hair was a thing. He was in full sunlight, so his squint wasn't unreasonable, but knowing that he beat my mother caused me to see his beady eyes as menacing. I took an immediate dislike to him, although there was nothing overtly threatening in the image. Gordon is in a couple of the pictures; he's about four years old, and he, Eugene, and Mom appear to be picnicking at the side of a lake.

What gets my attention is that in three of the pictures, with Gordon nowhere in sight, my mother is acting noticeably risqué. By today's standards, the photos are quite tame, but back when they were taken, in the era of Bettie Page and Vargas girls, my mother is giving her husband a little something to think about. With her halter top unbuttoned and her cleavage showing, she looks like a girl playing pin-up on a dare.

I don't think of myself as a prude. I had gone thru the Madonna "Like a Virgin" bustier phase. But this was *my mother* being sexy, and I couldn't handle it. It felt voyeuristic to look at those teaser pictures, and I quickly put them back in the envelope and didn't look again for many years. I was on a quest, but apparently there was a limit to how far I would go in violating my mother's privacy. These were her pictures to share, and I felt I was overruling that proprietary right. She may have shown them to me one day, but she died before that day could come. Walking the line between discovery and disrespect was one I would have to balance going forward; I needed to tread lightly.

As it happened, a couple of months after developing my mother's negatives, I was invited to a dear friend's wedding in Puerto Rico. I was concerned about how I might get through my first wedding without the libations. It defied my imagination how one might participate in a champagne toast without champagne, much less avoid the guests-getting-hammered routine, which seemed as much a part of the wedding ritual as the bride tossing her bouquet. What saved me was that my flight home was going to touch down in St. Louis, and St. Louis is a couple hours' drive from Decatur, Illinois, where my mother grew up. From my mother's strongbox, I found an old Christmas card from her pen pal Shirley Stanton. Using the return address, I sent a letter introducing myself and asking if she would meet with me. What came back was an enthusiastic "Yes!" She insisted that I spend a couple of my nights with her and her husband in their home. With the Stantons' invitation on the horizon, I was able to attend my friend's Caribbean wedding and join in the celebration without so much as a sniff of liquor. The Stantons had been my mother's friends, but mostly I was desperate to find out what they knew about my father. Meeting them was too important for me to risk getting sucked back into my booze habit.

Shirley and John Stanton were lovely Midwesterners. Their home was decorated with bowling trophies, crocheted Afghan throws, and maple furniture. They both couldn't get over how much I looked and sounded like my mother. I didn't think so, but they were floored. It was clear to me that my presence had caused them both to time-travel back to the old days, remembering people, places, and things that they had not considered for years.

When I asked Shirley and John, point-blank, if they had known Gerrick Abbott, they said that they didn't know much except that he was married. They shook their heads and pursed their lips, offering nothing new on that score. I was mindful of being up against a generation of folks, born in the 1930s, who took the concept of not airing dirty laundry as a personal credo.

I was disappointed to learn nothing new about Gerrick Abbott; he hadn't been the boy in the 1947 pictures. On day two of my visit, I started asking about my mother's family. I asked Shirley if she had known my mother's parents, and what did she know about the whole question of my mother being adopted or not? Shirley sighed a long sigh and then shook her head in consternation. She couldn't find any delicate way to put it, so she simply said that she didn't think my mother had ever been adopted. She said something like, "You know, Birdie (my maternal grandmother's nickname) was known to be a rounder, and I think your mother was just too embarrassed to admit she was her daughter."

"A rounder? What's that?"

John wasn't in the room, so perhaps Shirley was a little more at ease to get into it, but she was still quite circumspect with her choice of words. She described how she and my mother would ride their bikes over to the seamy side of town where my mother's mother lived. I found out that my grandparents had divorced, which I imagined must have been scandalous at the time. Shirley went on to tell me that Birdie could often be found in a bar, and she confessed that it was exciting to go there because of how naughty it was. Her parents would have "raised hell if they found out," she said. She told me how my grandmother would always be happy to see the two girls and would buy them each a bottle of Coca-Cola. I can't remember if Shirley called the place a cathouse or a honky-tonk or a speakeasy, but she made sure I understood that Birdie had a bedroom upstairs from the bar. I later learned that "a rounder" was a slang expression used to describe a person who was "dissolute or morally unrestrained." The word connoted someone who spent so much time lying on her back that her heels had no reason to compress flat; they'd be round. Basically, "rounder" was a euphemism for prostitute.

Shirley told me that Birdie had died in that bar, literally dropped dead off her barstool. I was both staggered and not surprised. That my grandmother drank herself to death was not that remarkable; I had basically seen my mother do it, and I had quit because I was afraid I might go down that same path. What took me aback was that it was sounding like my grandmother might have supported her habit by the oldest profession available to women. No wonder my mother had so little to say about her childhood. Whatever had occurred back then, it had to have been rough. My poor grandmother; what must *her* life have been like, I wondered. I didn't think of her as a disgrace; I had to imagine how few options a divorced female alcoholic in the 1930s and '40s must have had—to make *that* choice. Instead, I was overwhelmed by a deep sense of compassion.

What Shirley told me next nearly knocked me off my own stool. She said that after all the decades that had gone by, that notorious whorehouse had just burnt to the ground the week before my arrival. Spooky and far-fetched as it may sound, my immediate thought was that the brothel fire had been for my benefit. I formulated a notion that my mother and grandmother had made the decision, from within the spirit world, that I could have a glimpse into their pasts, but I didn't need to rub my nose in the stench. For whatever reason, I had been spared the full impact of their dark days. I had been the fortunate one, and suddenly, I felt a profound responsibility to the women who came before me. My sobriety was no longer just for me; it was for all three of us. I had made it out of the disease alive, but they hadn't. I could turn their shortcomings into my own strength.

Shirley could see that I was working all of this out in my mind. She asked me if I wanted to visit the cemetery where my grandmother had been buried, and I most certainly did. It hadn't occurred to me that Birdie Bierman would have been buried in Decatur, but only because I hadn't thought that far ahead.

That afternoon Shirley drove me to Graceland Forever Beautiful Cemetery. The secretary produced a file that contained handwritten information on heavy card-stock paper. Her old record, the cursive script full and florid, was a treasure trove of information, and I asked for a photocopy.

What I learned, for the first time, was that my grandmother had the same first name as my mother: Margaret. Margaret Bird Bierman had died at the age of forty-two on July 6, 1948. My mother had died at the age of forty-three. I was sixteen at the time; my mother would have been not quite fifteen when *her* mother died. My mother's name was listed at the top of a column meant for survivors' names and relationships. That's where I discovered the first names of my mother's aunts and uncles: James of Rochester, Earl of Louisville, Roy of Mason, Ted of Freeport, Isaac of Payne, Mrs. Ella Poe of Newton, Virginia, and Mrs. James Everett of Decatur. At the bottom of the record, my fourteen-year-old mother was listed as the person who would be responsible for the funerary services bill, which made me gulp and question why none of the brothers or sisters or some other adult would pay. There was more to that story, there had to have been, but neither Shirley nor the secretary could shed any light on the subject.

I left Decatur with too many emotions to sort out. I didn't know if I was happy or sad. I had been hungry for information, which I got, but I wasn't satisfied; in fact, I felt even hungrier than before. I had two more cemeteries to visit before getting on my plane for home: Valhalla, where I knew my grandfather was buried, and Lake Charles Burial Park. I had found receipts for those cemeteries in my mother's strongbox. Shirley thought Lake Charles might be where my grandfather's second wife was buried.

The Valhalla office was only able to provide me with a map of their grounds and an X on the plot where I would find my grandfather's final resting place. While standing at the site, I took a photo of his gravestone. It had a cast bronze plaque embedded in granite with no epitaph, only his name and the dates of his birth and death: February 14, 1898, and May 9, 1965. I was not aware that his birthday had been on Valentine's Day, but I was acutely aware that my mother had died on February 13. She was present in my thoughts, but I couldn't tell if it was because I was supposed to be on that hallowed ground or because I *wasn't*. Would she have been proud of me for my sleuthing or ashamed of me for not minding my own business? I wasn't sure if I should feel righteous or guilty. I was inserting myself in a past that both did and didn't belong to me. I didn't know these people, but if they were my mother's true biological parents, then they were also my grandparents, and I had a right to know something of them, didn't I?

I drove my rental car on to Lake Charles Burial Park. With my receipt dated May 22, 1948 in hand, I approached the front desk and asked if they could tell me anything about it. The secretary remarked on its age and stepped away for a few minutes, leaving me to take in the stifling placidity of that somber business. When she returned, she informed me that the receipt was for two plots, but only one was being used. She went on to say that it contained the remains of a Mrs. Mavis Louella Bierman. So that was the name of Grand-dad Bierman's second wife. Mavis, she said, died on May 21, 1948. That date meant that she had died less than two months before Margaret Birdie. Granddad had lost his first and second wives in very short order. The lady in the office told me that the second plot was available for sale, and that interested parties were to contact Margaret G, my mother. She produced a grounds map and put an X in the section where the two plots were, but she also informed me that no marker had ever been placed at either site.

Right away my mind started racing. I had gone to Illinois with one most pressing question: What did the Stantons know about my father? I hadn't gotten any answer on that front, but by the end of the trip, questions about my *mother* and her family had multiplied. Why didn't my mother live with her father and stepmother? What personal history had she labored under when she got involved with whoever got her pregnant with me? I could look back on my own relationships, where I hid so much of myself, and I wondered if my mother had done the same. What did my father know or not know about my mother? Did he ever meet *her* father? How had Helmut and Birdie met? Why did they get divorced? Was it her drinking? Who was the second wife? Why had Helmut not put a marker on Mavis Louella's gravesite, and why, seventeen years later when he passed away, was he not buried next to her? Why had he bought two plots at Lake Charles but ended up in Valhalla?

The list of questions kept growing.

I returned home feeling like a zombie. Learning something

about my mother as a young woman seemed relevant, but I still couldn't connect all the dots. In the places where there were gaps, I was doing nothing more than guessing about those people and events. So I decided to keep going.

Using my newly discovered names and birth and death dates, I sent inquiry letters requesting records from both Illinois and Missouri Health Department Vital Records Divisions. Helmut Bierman's death certificate arrived first. It told me that he was a United States citizen, what his parents' names were, and that he had died from "acute myocardial failure," or a heart attack. It also told me that he had been a "postal employee." Because he had been a federal worker, I then wrote to the National Personnel Records Center requesting his work history file. Next came Birdie's death certificate. It confirmed that she had died in a "public place." The coroner's report indicated that the cause of death was "cirrhosis of the liver, arteriosclerotic heart disease, multiple infarctions of left kidney, with acute cardiac collapse." Birdie's mother and father were listed as Isaac Landau and Eveline Pridemore.

When Granddad Bierman's employment record arrived, I learned that he had a forty-two-year career working in the railway mail service, receiving several promotions along the way. His only hiatus from postal work was during WWII when, in October of 1942, as a forty-four-year-old man, he enlisted as a naval reservist and was immediately put on active duty. His record stated that he was honorably discharged from military service on May 2, 1945, and two weeks later, on May 16, he was sworn back in as a railway postal clerk.

Digging further into his file, I found a section from the FBI. The top of the page indicated that it was a "Report on Loyalty Data," dated February 28, 1948. That would have been when J. Edgar Hoover was director of the FBI and during a time when the US House of Representatives had created HUAC, the House Un-American Activities Committee, which investigated private citizens across America for any behavior that could be viewed as disloyal to the country. Granddad's FBI report was stamped in the "No Derogatory Information Developed" box.

That an FBI report on my grandfather existed at all was bizarre, but what caused me to stop in my tracks was the report's box #10. It was reserved for the spouse's name, and there I read "Mavis Louella Bierman (née Landau)". Landau was Birdie's maiden name! That meant that Granddad Bierman's two wives were either related or it was a wild coincidence that they would both have the same maiden names. When Mavis's death certificate arrived and I saw that her parents were also Isaac Landau and Eveline Pridemore, I realized that Granddad's two wives had been sisters. Mavis Louella was born in the year 1900, making her the older sister by six years. She was two years younger than Helmut; Birdie would have been eight years younger than him.

My head wanted to explode, but I wasn't the exploding type; instead, I was *imploding*. It was all too much: LG and my mother, my mostly estranged siblings, my failed love life, my absent father, my grandparents' mysteries, staying sober in a drinking world; all these pressing issues made me feel like I was walking in mud. I continued to put on a happy face at work, but I was overwhelmed, and the day came when the seams split.

I was juggling a couple of customers at work when I stepped wrong and twisted my ankle. I went down, and there was no standing back up. My coworkers got ice and finished my customers, and a couple of times, I was asked if I wanted a glass of wine to ease my pain. A glass of wine never sounded better, but those same coworkers were aware that I was trying not to drink, and I didn't want to fall off the wagon in front of them. Instead, I started plotting how I was going to get drunk in secret.

I had given up cocaine, cigarettes, and alcohol all on the same day, figuring that I would be miserable so I might as well get it all out of my system at once rather than suffer through three different withdrawals. I gave them up together, and they all came back together. My thinking went, *Hell, I'm going to be off work until I can stand without crutches, so I'll have time to really tie one on. So go ahead and stop at the liquor store on your way home. Pick up a fifth of gin, some tonic and limes, and a pack of smokes, and then stop by the dealer's house to buy some cocaine.* Boom, boom, boom, I was ready.

But then another thought came to me. I remembered that Helen had told me, while I was still living in her pristine home, about a therapist. Although I was planning my big fat party of one, I still had enough control over my actions that I decided that I could call that person first. I would tell her what my drinking history had been, and if she didn't think I had an alcohol problem, I would go ahead with my bender.

I called Helen, and she called the therapist. The therapist called me, and the next day I was in therapy. Gwyndolyn was her name. I had no intention of lying to her, and I was still so deluded about my alcoholism that I honestly thought she would green-light my drinking without hesitation. I didn't think I was *that* bad. The thing was, Gwyndolyn didn't give me a pass. She turned out to be an expert in addiction.

She suggested that I start by telling her why I was concerned about my drinking. I told her about my mother dying young and that I had recently learned that my grandmother also had an early death related to alcohol abuse. That opened the door for more discussion about my family. "Family of origin" was the phrase she used. She wanted to know about my people, who I had come from. I told her that I had almost no information about my father. I justified his absence as understandable because I was illegitimate, as if that put an end to it. I told her what I had just discovered about my probable grandmother and grandaunt being sisters and marrying the same man. I briefly described my siblings and where I fell in the sibling order. I didn't hold back on my description of LG and why he was the root of all evil. She nodded her head and may have jotted down a few notes and asked a few questions, but for the most part, she was just taking me in.

She earned my confidence and respect right away because she didn't make nice; she was a no-nonsense person intent on making me well, even if healthy didn't actually mean happy, or at least not in the short term. She fully grasped that I was there with a problem, and she had gotten right to it. Although my family history sounded like a miserable tale of woe, I tried to deflect its gravity by speaking in a dismissive voice, like it was old news and I was over it, but Gwyndolyn was focused on both what I had to say and what my body was telling her. She took note of how shallow my breaths were, how hunched my shoulders were, and of how deep the frown lines were between my brows. She also noticed that my arms were wrapped across my gut and that, without even realizing it, I was rocking back and forth as I spoke. My words were telling her that it was all no big deal, but my body was crying out for help.

I began therapy with Gwyndolyn once a week for almost two years. Before leaving her office on that first day, I asked her again if she thought it would be okay for me to start drinking. She didn't sugarcoat her answer. She didn't give me any of that stuff about how only the individual can say for sure if they are an alcoholic or not. She said that, given all I had told her, if I continued to drink, "it will be like putting a gun to your head."

But she *didn't* tell me that I was a wreck and should be ashamed of myself. She *didn't* tell me that I was sentenced to daily penance for all my past misdeeds. And she didn't snatch the reins of my life to lead me around like a broken horse. She said it was up to me how I was going to kick the habit, but she encouraged me to check out Alcoholics Anonymous and Narcotics Anonymous. She also suggested the names of a couple of homeopaths and herbalists who could help strengthen my liver, and she floated the idea of joining a Native American–style drumming circle. Or perhaps the Sierra Club might have some activities that would interest me. What she said was, "You need to keep more sober company." Before scheduling my next appointment, she put the book *It Will Never Happen to Me!* by Claudia Black in my hand. It was subtitled: "Children of Alcoholics, As Youngsters-Adolescents-Adults."

When I got home, I literally threw up. Then I took a shower, put on warm pajamas, ate some real food, and started reading my new book about people just like me.

I was in therapy when I made my second foray into Mr. Abbott's life. In counseling, I was learning about myself, gaining insights into my vulnerabilities and the triggers that sent my self-esteem into a nosedive. Gwyndolyn had me reading self-help books on drug and alcohol addiction, sex and love addiction, perfectionism, and codependency. She and I would discuss how they made me feel, which was mostly wretched. My perfection seeking had less to do with any kind of external aesthetic of visual proportion and balance, and more to do with an unrealistic, idealized, emotional Zen, a state of mind I believed I could achieve if I could only figure out what I had done wrong. I gave a lot of thought to the idea of internalized shame and blame, and I came to see how my own psychological makeup drove me to respond in situations, especially out-of-control situations, by making them all about myself. As a child, I found it more acceptable to make myself wrong than to hold those who were supposed to care for me responsible. As an adult, I was doing the same thing. If I could make a problem *my problem* then I might be able to manipulate it, turn it into something I could control. I'd fix the car, pay the bill, or make the difficult phone call for other people, just because I couldn't stand the chaos of their own making. That defense became an unconscious pattern that I needed to unlearn. I was holding more than my fair share of guilt, and it became my job to stop seeing life in terms of right or wrong, good or bad, black or white, all or nothing. I had to figure out what was my business and what wasn't.

I stayed friendly with my drinking buddies, but I wasn't that same old party gal I had been; I learned to bow out early when the evening revved up. With a little effort, I cultivated a community of sober friends, my *sobies*, as I called them. They understood how it felt to walk past liquor bottles and have them jump off of the shelf and do a little cancan dance in the aisle. We could laugh at our crazy justifications for getting drunk and support each other in the one-day-at-a-time lifestyle. Cutting the future into twenty-four-hour segments took away some of the anxiety about never drinking for the rest of my life: all I had to worry about was the day I was in. We sobies met up frequently to affirm the need to stay away from that seductive first drink, because it only takes the first sip to wake the thirsty beast inside of us. I didn't ever want to go back to my booze habit. For me, there was no situation so bad that a drink couldn't make it worse, and no celebration that booze couldn't sour.

During my two-year period with Gwyndolyn, I picked up the pace and caliber of college courses I was taking. I signed up for a class on contemporary women writers that exposed me to female authors such as Tillie Olsen, Grace Paley, and Toni Cade Bambara. I was challenged to think about the role of women in our culture: what was valued, what was dismissed, and why. The more I learned about patriarchal rule, the more incensed I became about how men continued to benefit from the social, political, financial, and religious structures they created eons ago. My burgeoning cultural awareness added fuel to that unquenched subject that could flair up with the slightest provocation: Who was my father, and where was he? Why, I wondered, why was it not a capital crime for men to abandon their children? If men had been the bearers of off-spring, I have no doubt that the penalties for maternal neglect would be stiff and swift.

Fortified by a supportive community of friends and stoked with indignity, I decided to go after Mr. Abbott one more time. I hired a private investigator to find out where he worked. I thought a PI could tail him and get me an alternate address, a workplace where I could send another letter, since I was never sure he had gotten the one I sent to his home. I also wasn't 100 percent certain Mr. Abbott was my father, but he was involved with my mother for one reason or another, so he knew something, and I desperately wanted whatever information he could give me.

I found someone in the telephone directory who advertised that he specialized in missing persons, but when I showed up at his office, he did not inspire confidence. He was no Raymond Chandler or Dashiell Hammett, although he did have a bottle of Kessler's whiskey in his desk drawer that he offered to share with me. I declined but encouraged him to go ahead; he was a little shaky and looked like he would function better after a shot. His disheveled third-floor, walk-up office in the run-down section of downtown Oakland made me think I was the first client he had seen in a long time. He had to find a pen to write with, and then a tablet to write *on*. To clear his desk of dusty papers, he just swept them into a box he pulled out of a waste bin. My dusty detective wanted a couple hundred bucks, half of which I had to pay on the spot. As I left his office I thought, either he will find something, or I just gave away cold cash to a con man.

It took a few days, but the whiskey-drinking detective did come through. A third of what he turned over ended up being inaccurate, but he gave me two promising leads, addresses in the neighboring city of San Leandro: one for a bar called Gerry's Cocktail Club that was owned by Gerrick Abbott, and the other for Gerrick Abbott Jr.—the son born two months after my brother.

I hadn't been aware of that shortened version of Mr. Gerrick

Abbott's name, but on sight, I recognized that it might explain why my own name is spelled as it is. My birth name is Terry, not Teresa, and not the more feminine Terri. Perhaps the similar spellings, Terry and Gerry, were clues my mother planted, but then again, perhaps I was just grasping at straws.

I wanted to see this Gerry's Cocktail Club, even though I wasn't ready to recalibrate the professional standing I had imagined for Mr. Abbott. I told myself the bar must have been a shrewd business investment. I took a drive to the nearby city to poke around a bit. It was only about a half hour from where I was living. From the outside, Gerry's looked like nothing special—one door, no windows, stuck in the middle of a block on a long stretch of boulevard that was meant mostly for cars. It looked like the kind of place where LG and my mother would drink. It was also the kind of watering hole I used to drink in with my old drinking buddies. We thought it was great fun to go into those smelly, dark bars to play pool, feed quarters into the jukebox, and drink with the old-coot alkies. We young punks would be entertainment for the has-been regulars. I was well aware that by walking into Mr. Abbott's bar, I would be as conspicuous as a chief of police in full body armor. There would be no way to conduct a private conversation; eavesdropping and gossip could be high sport in those places.

So I drove away figuring I would craft another letter, a better letter, and send that one to the bar. This time I included a recent picture of myself. I figured it wouldn't hurt for him to see that I was a nice-looking young lady and not some crazy wild child. I also thought that if I bore any family resemblance, he might be moved to see his offspring. Despite my uncertainties, I wrote the letter as if Mr. Gerrick Abbott was indeed my father. I also decided to tell him that my mother had died. Maybe her passing might cause him to feel differently about talking to me. Plus, with my mother out of the picture, perhaps his wife would feel less threatened. With an embarrassing amount of newly learned vocabulary and marginally improved grammar and spelling, I typed the following on November 14, 1989, and included my current address and phone number:

Dear Gerrick,

As you might imagine any child would, I have an enormous amount of curiosity about you. I would like very much to meet you. I have known where you lived for many years. Recently I hired a Private Investigator to follow you; I asked him to find a way for me to contact you outside of your wife's knowledge, and that is what lead me to Gerry's Cocktail Club.

I have enclosed a recent photograph of myself. If it's true what they say, that "a picture is worth a thousand words," then I hope you can tell by it that you have nothing to fear in me. If you are agreeable, I can meet you, one morning or afternoon, at your bar. Just name the date and time and I'll be there.

Sincerely, your daughter

P.S. It is germane to note that my mother died thirteen years ago.

P.S.S. It would mean the world to me to have a photograph of you, if you can manage it, would you please bring one along?

Impatient to get the ball rolling and still unaware of the return receipts service at the post office, I dropped my fishing letter into a mailbox and began another anxious wait.

As I waited for a reply, I was concerned that my burgeoning resentments against men in general might show. I wasn't disgusted with Mr. A for possibly having an affair with my mother. I understood from my own love affairs that attraction, affection, and commitment did not always fall into tidy little boxes. I also had the benefit of birth control to prevent the creation of babies and to avoid social stigmatizing. So I accepted the fact that my parents' sexual conduct could have gotten very complicated very quickly.

But I was annoyed by Mr. A's inaccessibility, and I was afraid he would brush me off as just some crabby chick with a chip on her shoulder. So I kept trying to imagine his point of view. Maybe he had a perfectly good reason for wanting nothing to do with me. Maybe something bigger than an extramarital affair had occurred between him and my mother. Maybe my mother had been a stalker (though if so, why would he send checks?). Who knew what minefields I might be stepping into?

Every day for a couple of weeks, I eagerly checked my mailbox and jumped whenever my phone rang. I even kept an eye out for a covert spy. I had hired a PI to scout Mr. Abbott, so he could have done the same to me. But there was nothing. Chances were growing that I was truly being rejected, but I still held on to a thread of hope that somehow my letter had gotten into the wrong hands, had been lost in the mail, or had been overlooked by accident. If I had gotten a letter saying that he was not the person I thought he was and to leave him alone, I would have been less able to convince myself that some terrible misunderstanding had occurred. I would have stopped daydreaming that he was my father or that he wanted to find me as much as I wanted to be found.

Nothing, nothing, nothing came, but unwilling to be denied, I ratcheted up more nerve, drove to his house, and knocked on his front door. I was possessed. I didn't care what happened. I just wanted anything but the silence.

Pressing a doorbell never took as much strength as it did on the morning I marched to the Abbotts' front door and went for it. Mrs. Abbott was the one to answer. I'm sure she thought I was there to peddle magazine subscriptions or solicit some kind of donation. She was taken aback momentarily when I told her that I was Terry G and wanted to know if Mr. Gerrick Dean Abbott lived there. With understandable hesitation, she said that yes he lived there, but he wasn't home at the moment. I asked her if she knew who I was, and she said she did. Conceding to the moment, she said I could come inside.

Mrs. Abbott looked like the type of mom who would bake cookies, go to PTA meetings, and belong to a bowling league, which is to say, she didn't seem threatening in any way. She was dressed in polyester slacks and a floral-print blouse. She was fully made up, and her hair was done in a roller-set style. She was polite and in no way hostile toward me. As she ushered me to a family room, we walked through her living room. The home was decorated in a style similar to Shirley Stanton's in Decatur: glass-topped coffee tables, knickknacks, recliners, an overstuffed couch.

I was struck by the massive family portrait that hung over the fireplace. It disturbed me on sight. Proud of their brood and smiling, Mr. and Mrs. Abbott huddled together with their three spunky children: two boys and a girl. It was immediately clear that Mr. Abbott was my brother's father. Sean looked just like the man framed in that photo. In fact, Sean looked more like Mr. Abbott than his two legitimate sons did. The happy family tableau turned my stomach. It was jealousy; I knew it. I longed for one of those close-knit families that hung pictures of their enviable lives around a house that was kept clean enough for strangers to be invited in without embarrassment. But Mr. Abbott could hang all the dignified portraits he wanted; from that moment on, I would know that he had abandoned at least one of his children, my brother Sean. I didn't see much to convince myself that he was *my* father, but because Sean and I looked alike—when we were young, we could pass for twins—maybe he was, which made talking to his wife all the more odd.

Mrs. Abbott and I sat in a less formal room off the kitchen. She positioned herself next to me on a couch. Sitting so close to the lady, *that lady*, made me feel very strange. She had every right to treat me with contempt, but she didn't. She wasn't effusive, but she wasn't rude either. I struggled to get my bearings. For a brief moment, my mother and grandmother popped into my head. I imagined them watching me, sending me the guts to carry on while at the same time shaking their heads at my folly.

To initiate some conversation, I asked Mrs. Abbott if I could call her by her first name. She said of course I could, so I then had to ask her what it was. She said, "It's Margaret." I may have flinched, but I tried not to give anything away. She and my mother had the same first name! Yes, it was a common one, but that coincidence threw me further off-kilter. I had to wonder how Mr. Abbott dealt with it; maybe he used special pet names to distinguish the two? This odd coincidence added another hundred pounds to the elephant in the room.

If Mr. Abbott was in fact my father, I really didn't want to hear about it from his wife. She was a nice lady, but I had gone to that house wanting to get answers from him, not her. I couldn't fathom how Margaret Abbott could explain an affair her husband had with my mother, an affair that lasted long enough to possibly produce two children. She had to have been pissed. So, I held my cards close to the vest, and she basically did the same, which gave us very little to talk about. I didn't let on about the gut-punch I felt from seeing Mr. Abbott in the family portrait. And I didn't tell her that she had the same name as my mother, but it was almost all I could think about.

Preoccupied with a host of intrusive thoughts, I angled for some extra time by bringing up a topic that played well with hair salon customers: her children. Mrs. Abbott picked up the subject without hesitation and informed me that her oldest, Joanne, lived in Washington State, had married straight out of high school, had a daughter, and went to church regularly. I told Mrs. Abbott that I didn't attend any churches. That, in turn, allowed her to express her own misgivings about religion. The upshot, however, was that her daughter was an adult with a mind of her own, and what she chose to do with her time was her own business. About Mrs. Abbott's sons, I learned that Gerrick Jr. was married, and he and his wife had just had their first baby. About her youngest child, another son, she said he was the rebel, and he was the one that gave her the most grief, a tossed-out revelation she expressed with a slight chuckle.

It was interesting to me that she wasn't bragging about her kids. Her love was obvious, but she seemed more comfortable talking about their flaws than singing their praises. I attributed her candor to the fact that they were all grown and out of the house by the time we were sitting together. Her job raising them was over, and how they behaved as adults had nothing to do with her personally. Or maybe she didn't want to give the impression of being too proud. Whatever it was, it made me think that I could maybe fit in one day. Maybe they weren't the hoity-toities I had always assumed them to be.

I asked Mrs. Abbott if she thought Mr. Abbott might be back anytime soon, and she seemed surprised. "Oh, no," she said. Then she explained to me that Mr. Abbott didn't drive. He worked with their son Gerrick Jr., and Junior wouldn't bring him back until later in the afternoon. The notion that father and son worked together yanked my chain some more. I couldn't imagine anything better than being in a family that pulled together like that. I was flush with envy and the feeling of being an outsider.

I saw Mrs. Abbott as the fortress guard, dispensing information as she alone saw fit. She showed no overt signs of animosity toward me, but she also wasn't asking any questions or showing any interest in my history or me. As time was passing, I began to wonder if she was being just as poker-faced as I was. The game had me wanting in and her wanting me out. Each move seemed strategic and covert. My incursion was being tolerated, but she gave no reason for me to be encouraged. In my mind, I thought she was playing it cool. I also thought of myself as the mistake that needed to be swept under the carpet. The polite parlor talk was just a ruse.

I was tumbling off track with a head full of conflicting thoughts. I wanted to leave Mrs. Abbott with a favorable impression, since I wanted her to convince Mr. Abbott to meet me. But I was also fuming; I was sure she knew more than she was letting on, and it was clear she had no intention of calling her husband home from work to meet with me. I still wanted to get to know these people, but to prepare myself for rejection, I was already telling myself that they weren't so great. Mr. Abbott probably didn't drive because he had been a drunk driver and had his license revoked, probably one of those drunk drivers who gets off light because of his status as an establishment white male. Who needed them anyway?

As my uninvited appearance was wearing thin, I asked Mrs. Abbott if her husband had recently received my letter and picture. She seemed to know nothing of it. I was glad because it gave me one leg up. I wanted to say, "I know something you don't." But really, it was pathetic. All I had was one stealthy letter to a bar; she had the man himself.

I was at her house for less than an hour when I got the sense that I was being dismissed. She asked if there was anything else, which sounded to me like, "We're done here, now move along." I didn't understand anything about where I stood. This ending felt abrupt, as if I had been interviewing for a job that I wasn't going to get. But I wasn't done. I told her that I remembered that when I was growing up, my mother had gotten checks from Mr. Abbott every month, and I would like to talk to him about them. Mrs. Abbott almost didn't let me finish my sentence before she was correcting me. She wanted me to know, in no uncertain terms, that Mr. Abbott had never sent my mother anything; *she* had.

I almost couldn't believe it. *She* was the one who had sent those checks every month? But then I remembered always admiring the beautiful penmanship on the checks. It was part of why I had elevated Mr. Abbott to such lofty heights; I thought he must be really smart and disciplined to have such elegant penmanship. So why didn't I ask Mrs. Abbott right then and there to explain what those checks were all about? All I can say is that I didn't want to hear what went on between Mr. Abbott and my mother from *her*.

Also, the image I had held of Mr. Abbott all my life was quickly crumbling. His non-reply to my letters and my mother's note, his pleased-with-himself expression in the family portrait, the fact that his wife and lover had the same name, and then the knowledge that he hadn't even been the one to send us that money propelled my thoughts into overdrive. It was already way more than I could take in.

I was ready to leave, but before going, I reiterated my desire to meet with her husband, and she assured me that she would tell him I had come by. She even said one of them would call me the next day.

efore the sun went down that same day, I made another
trip to San Leandro on the off chance that Gerrick Jr.
might talk to me. I didn't have high hopes of breaking through
to Mr. Abbott by Mrs. Abbott's efforts alone. I wondered if by
meeting one of his children and showing him that I presented
no threat, together we could get the vault that contained the
story of my birth to unlock.

As I drove, I rehearsed what I would say and do. I was
counting on common decency from Junior, but I understood
that there was a chance it might not go well. Cold-calling was
never fun, but I was going to steel myself against whatever
came of it. I'd get right to it: tell him my name, tell him that I
had just met his mother, and let him know there was a chance
that we had the same father. Once that was done, either he
would talk to me or he wouldn't. Since I didn't have a phone
number, there was no way around yet another front door to
knock on with the hope that it wouldn't be slammed in my
face. By then, I weighed risk and reward, and figured nothing
ventured, nothing gained. I wanted to go to sleep that night
knowing that I had really tried everything to get Mr. Abbott
to talk to me.

Junior answered the door with his infant daughter resting
at his shoulder. He was a proud papa, and before he had any
reason to put his guard up, there was a brief, pleasant moment
in which we both seemed to pause in deference to the babe
in arms. It passed, and I launched into my practiced lines. He
raised his eyebrows, but he didn't tell me to go away. I asked
if he would please talk to me for just a few minutes. By then,
Junior's wife was at his side, and they looked questioningly

at one another. To my great relief, they let me in. As new parents, I think they were soft on the subject of children and family, so that helped me get my foot in the door.

We only talked for about half an hour. During that time, the sun had set and the interior of the small home was dark except for the kitchen where we sat. I sensed that the scene looked like something out of an Edward Hopper painting—gloomy despite the overhead lights. It was quite somber, and made all the more poignant by the newborn that slept in the shadows. I explained my plight to the couple, saying that my mother was no longer living and couldn't provide the answers I was after. Without any hard proof of paternity, I remained tentative in how I spoke about Mr. Abbott. I told Junior that every month, my mother received checks with Mr. Abbott's name on them, and I wanted to know why. I didn't mention my recent knowledge that Mrs. Abbott had written them, and I didn't say anything about his father's name being encoded on my birth certificate and my brother Sean's. If my gambit worked, there would be time to get into that sometime down the road.

Junior was refreshingly direct. He told me that he knew about the checks because he had seen them one day as a kid. His folks weren't home when he had gone riffling through their drawers and found the stack of cancelled checks written to my mother. He instinctively understood that Margaret G was a secret subject, so he never confronted his parents with his finding. Plus, he couldn't explain his snooping without getting himself into trouble, so he kept his discovery to himself all those years. He did admit to me, however, that he always thought it was hush money of some kind.

I was interrupting their dinner hour, but Junior and his wife didn't seem especially eager to be rid of me. They were cordial, just as Mrs. Abbott had been, but I didn't think that these strangers were simply being polite; I thought they were buying a little time to work out what my surfacing might mean in the long run. I got the sense that while we were all being amiable on the surface, in the back of our minds, each of us was calculating cost/benefit scenarios. But I almost felt a conspiratorial kinship was in the works; we were both after elusive answers to nagging questions.

Junior asked how old I was. I told him and then asked his age. He was three years older, just like Sean, his most-certain half brother. Junior and his wife gave no indication that they were aware of the indecorous detail of Mrs. Abbott and my mother being pregnant at the same time, so I stayed zipped up. I wasn't going to be the one to inform Junior that he had not been his father's firstborn son. Besides, given all I had learned that day, I couldn't say how many illegitimate children Mr. Abbott might lay claim to.

The remainder of our time together was filled mostly with the same kind of chitchat I would have in the hair salon with my customers. We each described our work. I learned that Junior had graduated from San Jose State and was now working in construction. Husband and wife talked about meeting and getting married; I told them I was single. Before I wore out my welcome, I wrapped things up by asking what I had gone there in the first place to ask: Would Junior tell his father that we met, and could he do anything to tip the scales on my behalf?

At that point, an expression crossed Junior's face that totally stunned me; it was dead-on one that both Sean and I make. I understood every fine sinew and muscular twitch of that look: it was one of annoyance about the absurdity of something that had just been said or suggested. From that facial ripple, I had no doubt that the guy sitting in front of me was indeed my relative, probably my half brother. But I also knew he was going to be of no help in getting his father to acknowledge that or contact me. He said that he and his father didn't have that kind of relationship, so no, he wouldn't be able to say a word to his parents.

I thanked Junior and his wife for their time and told them that I understood the difficulty I presented. I had never been able to confront *my* mother about uncomfortable things either. So when Junior said he couldn't step in, I could see that it was not because he didn't want to; it was because it was just too risky.

When my phone rang the next day, my hunch was that it would be one of the Abbotts, but I couldn't guess which one. I picked up the receiver hoping it would be Mr. Abbott, but it was only Mrs. Abbott. At the sound of her voice, my heart began what was becoming a familiar nervous gallop. Attempting to control my voice and seem breezy and light, my "Oh, hi!" sounded like something that came out of Minnie Mouse. From her tone, I got the impression that Mr. Abbott was not with her; I hated to think he would be standing by while she spoke for him. She was far more clipped than she had been the day before, and without wasting any time, she said, pretty much verbatim, and I'll never forget it:

"I spoke to Gerrick, and he wants nothing to do with you. He's concerned you are trying to get his children's inheritance. I asked him about the picture you sent, and he told me he threw it in the garbage."

I took that on the chin. Before hanging up, I let her know I was disappointed. In private, I ranted to the warm walls of my apartment. "Those people are seriously screwed up. I don't need to expose myself to their twisted values and abuse. *His* children? Excuse me. Do you hear yourself talking? *Inheritance*? He's the one with shaky principals, and you're going to twist that around to call *me* a gold digger! And why did she have to tell me that he threw my picture in the garbage? She just said that to hurt me! Hell, maybe it never even happened; maybe it's what she *wished* he had done. And what a creep, getting his wife to do his dirty work and tell me all this stuff. That family's problems are much bigger than mine, and I don't need their dysfunction."

Gwyndolyn and my friends helped me pull myself together in the immediate aftermath of that piercing disappointment. Mr. Abbott remained untouchable, but, crazy as it may sound, I maintained a scintilla of hope that he was still just in the dark. It was possible he hadn't received either of my letters, and his wife had said nothing to him about my visit. Junior easily could have been true to his word that he wouldn't confront his father. I didn't know this Mr. Abbott, but clearly he had a hold on the people around him—his secret keepers, including my mother.

Frustrated and powerless, I wanted to lash out, but I also wanted to curl up in the fetal position and cry myself to sleep—that night, and every night after that for quite awhile. It all hurt too much, and I had to get a grip. I understood that I was experiencing acute rejection because of having been abandoned, but in what felt like an epiphany, I realized that I was going to have to take responsibility for my own healing. In short, the love and understanding I craved was going to have to come from within. Expecting others to provide that nurture was like expecting someone else to lose weight for me. In my quest for some perfect ideal of a life, I had turned a blind eye to my more vulnerable feelings of grief and sorrow. What dawned on me was that I had to stop abandoning *myself*.

F ive years went by before I took another dip in the Abbott pool. I didn't have high hopes for a response, and I didn't get one, but by then, my life had smoothed out considerably, and I was better equipped to handle *that which I could not change*. During those intervening years, I had stayed sober, an effective antidote to low self-esteem. When I made the effort to pay attention to my own invalidating attitudes and behaviors, they changed, and I stopped being so blasted by events that resembled rejection.

Here's what else happened. Shortly after my face-to-face encounter with Mrs. Abbott and Junior, I made the decision to change salons where I worked. Memories of my Los Angeles fiasco still dogged me, but maturity in hairdressing typically means moving into "independent contractor" status. I had been an employee paid on a commission basis. If I wanted to take home a higher percentage of my earnings and not have to ask permission for vacation time, I'd have to go independent, to a salon that rented the styling chair and left all of the business management to each individual stylist. Since that wasn't offered in the salon where I was, I crossed my fingers and gave change another chance.

Breaking away from my colleagues was a decision I thought about long and hard. My coworkers had been a surrogate family to me for ten years, and when it was time to go out on my own, I was both excited and scared. My bosses didn't want me to leave, but they also wouldn't have dreamed of holding me back. They were more than just employers; they were caring friends. It was my choice to stick with what was comfortable or risk going into the unknown, and I decided I had to take the risk.

A new salon had opened up in Oakland, and a man who was known for bringing in good hairdressers with established clienteles owned it. In fact, a couple of stylists from Alexander Pope's had already gone over to his salon, and it was with their encouragement that I made the move.

As an independent, once I made the new salon's rent and expenses, the rest of my income was mine to keep. I was able to set my own prices, and the more efficiently I worked the more my income grew, to the point where I was able to work half as hard and make twice as much money. With that kind of financial security and extra time, I stepped up my education. I had been attending community college classes for almost ten years, and more and more I was being asked what I planned to do with all of those credits that I had been accumulating. My answer had been, "Nothing. I just like taking classes." But one afternoon, four-year university recruiters were on the junior college campus, and I ended up talking to a woman at the Mills College table. I took an application even though I didn't anticipate doing anything with it. For a couple of weeks, I tried to ignore the application, but it kept talking to me; it was saying, "Get me out of this drawer. You're going. You know you are going; now get me out of here and let's get on with it."

One of the more attractive aspects of Mills was that the classes would be small. It reminded me of the decision I made to work at Alexander Pope's instead of at a fancy San Francisco salon: at Mills I would be seen and held accountable. Also, I didn't want this next level of academic ambition to turn learning into a frantic competition to get into classes or capture the professor's attention. I wasn't going to school as a way of getting a job; I *had* a job. I was fortunate in that I was going to school for no other reason than personal edification.

The application I sent in did a fair job of expressing much of who I was as a student. I wanted to be honest, and I told myself that if I turned out not to be of Mills' caliber, so be it, but by then, I was dreaming about the beautiful campus and what it would mean to have a college degree. I really wanted into the school, so much so that I even asked my ex-boyfriend Aaron to talk to his mother. Aaron's mom had not only graduated from Mills College with a master's degree but was also her class's valedictorian. Her very kind letter back to me included a copy of the recommendation she had sent to the admissions office. She wrote that she believed in me and that I was mature beyond my years; she used the words "focused," "determined," "responsible," "consistently thoughtful," and "sensitive to others." Receiving such a glowing endorsement from a woman I looked up to gave my confidence a huge boost. I sent in the application package and waited with fingers crossed.

When the response came back, it read: "The answer is yes: we want you to be a Mills woman!" A significant door was opened to me, and I walked through. I signed up to be a full-time student because I couldn't get the financial aid needed to attend otherwise. I went in with enough community college credits that I was able to complete the requirements for a bachelor's degree within four semesters. Full-time meant four classes each semester. I had never worked and taken that many classes all at the same time, but I thought I could do it; I *had* to do it. By then I had signed numerous contracts and commitments for financial aid and student loans, and they all made it clear that if I didn't keep up my grades, or if I dropped out, I was going to have to pay all of the money back whether I received a degree or not.

My professors were brilliant, and the subjects were fascinating. I wasn't an academic superstar, but I didn't miss a day of instruction, and I turned in all of my assignments. As much as I would have enjoyed being a straight A student, I continually reminded myself that my ultimate goal was to stay in school long enough to get the degree. As far as I knew, I would be the first person in my family to graduate from college. I finished with a 3.356 grade point average in January of 1992. My declared major was English. It was a crowning achievement to go from so far behind, as a young nonreader, to getting a BA in English from one of the finest schools in the country.

Graduation day was golden. For the occasion, I reserved a picnic spot under a grove of eucalyptus trees on campus and threw myself a party. Mr. B and his new wife, Gwendolyn, Helen, Sean, a bunch of my friends and sobies, and Aaron and Susan were all there celebrating with me. Aaron and Susan had married and were expecting their first child. Since our early sex, drugs, and rock and roll days, we had all done a lot of growing up. I could see that, as a couple, they were far more suited for each other than he and I had ever been. It also didn't hurt that Aaron had stepped in and asked his mother if she would help me get into Mills College. Indelicate as their start had been, I no longer felt any need to hold Aaron's or Susan's feet to the licking flames of righteous indignation.

I'm glad I didn't, because Aaron turned out to play a major role in what would be the happiest and most transformative phase of my life. Not long after graduation, Aaron called and asked if I would be interested in going to Sears Point Raceway to watch him compete. Aaron and his father had gotten involved with Sports Car Club of America, an amateur, weekend auto-racing club that competes for trophies, not cash. Hanging out at the track on a sunny afternoon in the rolling hill of Sonoma sounded like a good time, so I signed on. I called a single girlfriend I had known since high school and asked if she wanted to go, telling her, "There will be lots of cute guys there," not realizing that her brother, Lutrell, would be one of them.

Lutrell is six months younger than I am, and when we were all in high school, I kind of thought he was a dork. He was in the grade below mine, and he was a painfully shy nerd who rarely spoke. He wasn't into any drinking or drugging. He didn't even smoke cigarettes, so that was way too square for my taste. But with five years of sobriety under my belt, seeing him at the racetrack, on his own turf, in his element, had me wondering. Was he really that same little brother? He was so mature, so handsome, so polite, and if he was still the straight arrow he had once been, that made him exponentially more interesting this time around. He was surprised to see his older sister at the track, but he perked up with delight at the sight of us. I watched, somewhat agog, as he spoke with complete ease, nothing like how I had remembered him. It turned out that he worked at the track as a mechanic for a race car driving school, and he had a race car of his own. He was also competing that day, but in a different category than Aaron. I learned that he had built his car from scratch, which was impressive. He was most definitely passionate about something I knew nothing about, and I was intrigued.

Lutrell needed to get his race car ready, so his sister and I went on to find Aaron and Susan. I didn't understand much about motor sports, or club racing, so after a few hours, without waiting to watch Lutrell compete, his sister and I left for the day. We hadn't been able to find him, so we left without even saying goodbye.

Although I had been happily single and not particularly eager to get involved with anyone, I kept thinking about Lutrell. I tried to picture the two of us dating. If things didn't work out—and I had little confidence in any relationship working out—I worried about the consequences for my friendship with his sister. It seemed risky. My dating record had not been pretty, and I didn't want either of us getting hurt. Furthermore, I knew that whoever came into my life as my next boyfriend would have to be serious. No longer was I going to waste time fooling around and playing the good-time gal. I was looking for an ocean of love, not another little pond. So if Lutrell was *the one*, I had to consider how it would feel to have my high school friend and her family as in-laws.

A couple months went by, and then Aaron happened to call a second time to let me know about another event at Sears Point. The invitation struck me as a gentle nudge to take a closer look at Lutrell. For that reconnaissance mission, I asked another girlfriend, and I told her what I was up to. She assured me that she didn't mind if we spent extra time talking to Lutrell.

We found him at the track in the same driving school's garage, attending to race day details. He recognized me right away and perked up just as he had with his sister. Making every attempt to appear casual, I asked as many questions as I could come up with about racing and his race car. Again, he was poised and considerate. I also noticed how patient and methodical he was in describing his particular style of car and why it was special. And he was a good listener, answering our questions with interesting facts and analogies. I didn't get the sense that he was flirting or trying to impress; he just knew his subject and was comfortable talking about it.

He wasn't wearing a ring, and I didn't notice any girls hanging around. And the more he talked, the more I hoped that it was because he *didn't* have a girlfriend. For the rest of the afternoon, I tried to pay attention to the racetrack activities, but I was definitely distracted. I still wasn't sure about getting involved with my friend's brother, but my heart was beginning to swoon.

Lutrell won his race that day, but it was the last race of the weekend, and while my friend had been a good sport about the long day, she was ready to head home. We stopped by the race school garage, but Lutrell wasn't there. I didn't realize that there was an entire process that took place after each race in which the event officials held the winning cars and drivers for post-race inspections. It pained me to leave the facility without congratulating Lutrell or saying goodbye, but that's what we did.

Driving away, I had that unmistakable feeling of attraction, but it wasn't the old glom-on-and-don't-let-go kind of feeling; I recognized that he was a different breed of cat, and I wanted to get to know him better. That evening, I called his sister. There was no way that I could initiate getting closer to Lutrell without having her blessing first. I told her that I had been to the raceway again that day, and with fingers crossed, I put my interest in her hands and said, "Your brother has become such a handsome man. I was wondering how you would feel about giving him my phone number?"

I don't think the idea had occurred to her, but I took it as a good sign that she didn't balk. In fact, she thought it was a good idea. I figured if she gave him my number and he didn't use it, I would be fine; I would know he wasn't interested. But I didn't want to put him on the spot by being the one to call first. I also wasn't going to make myself too easy. It's one thing to fall into a fellow's lap; it's another to wait for him to come around. Looking back on my previous relationships, I felt there had been an imbalance in them all. I jumped in too quick, doubting that any guy would ever have enough interest in me to make the first move. My fear had been if I didn't do the initiating, then I would be left out in the cold, forever alone. Allowing Lutrell the room to decide for himself what to do with my phone number was an act of faith, faith that if it was meant to be, then, it would be.

He called the next day. He was nervous; I could hear it in his voice. I congratulated him on his win at the raceway and complimented his driving. We mostly talked about the event, but as that subject was winding down, he asked how my day had been. Neither of us wanted to hang up, but it was getting to that point. I was hoping he would suggest a date of some kind, but it wasn't happening. It took conscious effort on my part not to leap in. There was some silence and awkward pauses, but I let them stand. I simply wasn't going to suggest the first date. We were doing more throat clearing than talking when he marshaled what I could hear was great courage, and ventured to ask if I would like to go with him to Laguna Seca Raceway in Monterey the next Saturday for another auto racing event. I got the sense that he held his breath waiting for my answer. I don't handle disappointment well—mine or anyone else's. It causes me actual physical distress. But I had to tell him I couldn't go. Saturdays were the busiest day of the week in the hair salon, and there was no way I could take a vacation day with so little notice. One of my clients was coming in for her wedding hairdo; it would be criminal for me to cancel on her.

Lutrell understood, but I could hear his chagrin. I absolutely didn't want to give the impression that I wasn't interested, so after he took a moment to absorb the rejection, I suggested meeting for a Sunday hike—and he thought that was a great idea. Lutrell lived in Sonoma and I lived in

Oakland, so I suggested a trail on Mt. Tamalpais, roughly half-way in between.

Sunday came, and we were going to meet up at a pullout along the highway and then drive together to the trailhead. The location was unmarked, but it was a spot where dozens of cars parked, and I thought it would be unmistakable. I arrived basically on time, but Lutrell wasn't there yet. I didn't panic, but I did start watching the clock. Ten minutes became twenty. At thirty minutes, I was giving up hope; at forty-five, I accepted that I had been stood up. I had no idea what could possibly have gone wrong, but rather than try to figure it out, I told myself to just drop it. It was a gorgeous a day for a hike, so I decided to go ahead and do the hike by myself.

I drove another couple of miles up the road, well over an hour past our assigned meet-up time, when I came upon a much larger paved municipal parking area. That's when I spotted Lutrell at a pay phone booth, with a panicked expression on his face. My description of the first parking lot and his understanding of the first parking lot had been two very different places. Neither of us had been wrong; it was an understandable mistake. At the sight of his visible distress and relief, I got the sense that he would have waited for me the entire day if he'd had to. It felt like a miracle that I had decided to go on the hike alone and not just head back home. It also felt miraculous that Lutrell hadn't given up. His willingness to wait for me spoke volumes to my tender heart.

We did the hike, a seven-mile loop down to the Pacific Ocean and back. We were together for several hours. He talked about racing and I talked about hairdressing. We told stories about our friends and the adventures we had with them. There were spells in the hike that went along in silence, admiring the scenery in mutual admiration for its beauty. I had packed a picnic lunch for the two of us, which we ate in the cove of a secluded beach with a world-class view of the Pacific. At the end of the day, back at our cars, we hugged but didn't kiss goodbye. The kissing came later.

Two years after that first hike, almost to the day, in September of '94, back at the same ocean cove, in a party of seventeen people including three of my best girlfriends, my brother Sean and his wife, Lutrell's mother, father, siblings, aunt, uncle, spouses and children, we got married.

Lutrell is my prince. Not a day goes by that I don't feel as though I have won the love lottery. He is a still-waters-run-deep kind of man who has eyes for me and me alone. We are best friends. On our second date, I told him that I was a sober alcoholic and that I hadn't had a drink in five years. If that was going to be a deal breaker, then I wanted to get it out of the way as soon as possible. He was visibly relieved to have the conversation. He's never been interested in getting loaded, and he remembered the kind of girl I had been in high school—and had concerns of his own.

I didn't let myself hide with Lutrell. It helped that we lived an hour's drive apart, because after that first date, we talked on the phone every night and were able to really get to know one another. I wanted him to know all of me so that I could trust that what we had was genuine.

On one of our first vacations together, we drove to Cambria, about a four-hour drive down the coast. Along the way, as he drove, I fell asleep with complete abandon. When I woke up, I couldn't believe how trusting I had become of the man at my side. I was letting my guard down, and that vulnerability has never been violated. As he drove, my race car driver obeyed every traffic rule and practiced every necessary caution to assure my safety. I had confidence that Lutrell had nothing to prove on public roadways. The competitor in him stayed at the raceway. He gave the other drivers a wide berth because he well knew that most people don't know how to drive. There's never any tailgating, flashing of headlights, swerve arounds, or hollering obscenities. Lutrell drove me to Cambria as if he was transporting precious cargo. I knew I had found *the one*.

After we returned from our honeymoon, I sent Mr. Abbott one of the leftover gold-embossed wedding announcements. On the back of it, I simply wrote, "Dear Gerrick Abbott, I don't want the fact that I have changed my name and address to prevent you from ever reaching out to me, should you have a change of heart. I would still like to meet you."

The post office didn't send it back with a "Return to Sender" stamped on it, so my assumption was that *someone* in his house had gotten it. By then I was thirty-four, and Mr. Abbott would have been almost sixty-three. The non-reply stung, but only a little. By then I thought that playing the I-don't-see-you game was rather juvenile, but *whatever*. I was married to someone I trusted; I had overcome so many of the sorrows from my past; I had moved to the beautiful Sonoma Valley and found a perfect salon to which many of my Oakland customers were happy to travel; I found sobies, and my heart was full of gratitude. Whatever was in Mr. Abbott's heart remained a mystery that I still wanted to uncover, but not with any strong-arm tactics. I got the sense that his demons were bigger than mine. My wedding announcement was a gentle reminder to him that I still wanted to meet, but I had to leave it at that.

Another nineteen years went by before I got a break. It had been right under my nose all along, in the strongbox. But before I move on to the next Abbott developments, there were several additional twists that occurred.

In 1996, my half sister Ellie gave birth to her third child, her second son. It was at that point she felt the need to find out what had become of her own father, LG. The last she knew of him, he was a homeless transient. During his demise, Ellie's grandmother, Mrs. G, had turned her back on both of them, and when Mrs. G died, she left nothing of her fortune to either her son or granddaughter.

Ellie had distanced herself from LG after he set fire to a residence hotel where they had been living in downtown Oakland many years earlier. She told me that she had contacted the last known social worker to handle his case, and he'd informed her that LG had died at a mental health facility the previous year. Ellie asked if I would take her to that facility so she could see, with her own eyes, what the place was like. It was going to be heavier for her than for me, but I wanted to know too; LG had been the male head of household for the first seventeen years of my life. I never thought of him as a father, but he was significant. Once we arrived at the mental hospital and signed a few forms, Ellie was handed a report, which painted a very disturbing picture.

The hospital's medical history revealed that LG had been "precipitously discharged" from a nursing home after he became "agitated" and "different." Upon admittance to the hospital where he died one month later, the report describes LG as "a very disheveled thin black male who opens his eyes to voice but will not follow any commands; he fights examiner when attempted to be touched or moved." LG was Caucasian but must have been so filthy that the reporter mistook his ethnicity. It goes on to describe his skin as "dirty, smelling of urine." Under the heading "Impressions," part of the admitting physician assessment reads in all capitals, "MALE WITH APPARENT CHRONIC SEVERE ORGANIC BRAIN SYNDROME, ETIOLOGY UNKNOWN." The doctor goes on to write, "patient was very combative for examination, kicking and pushing me away. He had poor dentition." Amidst several entries regarding medical tests and prescribed medication was a paragraph that read:

> We are told that because of the patient's behavioral disturbance he is not an acceptable candidate for nursing homes, which have refused his admission. I should state that while here he had exhibited intermittent bouts of combativeness and physical abuse to himself and to the staff. For example, he would grab people's wrists and turn them backward; he additionally grabbed a breast of a staff member with great force; he additionally grabbed the hair and began banging the head of a staff member against his own. It was felt that for the patient's safety as well as that of the staff's, that sedation was prudent.

The report described his "Social History" as "Not known." "The patient admits to alcohol abuse; however, he is not a reliable historian." In the neurological exam, LG was unclear about his name, his age, where he was, the year, or where he came from. When he was asked who the president was (Bill Clinton would have been the correct answer), he replied, "President Nixon's maiden name." It was also noted that he was eating with his fingers. His weight at one point was one hundred pounds. He had seizures, pneumonia, and urinary tract infections. It's stated in the report that the hospital was unable to contact any family. Under "Condition on Discharge," it only read: "Expired."

Ellie took in all of this with a stiff spine. The truth is, neither of us found anything shocking in the report. We knew about LG's psychiatric condition and had been unable to do anything about it. His death certificate led us to where he had been buried, presumably without ceremony. LG's social worker must have secured the burial plot with funds set aside from Mrs. G.

I did not feel good or redressed by any of this. LG's tragic ending was dismal, and I was pierced by the extraordinary arc of his life. He had been born to significant wealth and staunch Catholic parents, but that hadn't saved him from a life of extreme poverty, physical devastation, and mental isolation. I saw him as a man who played out his entire karmic package in one lifetime, both inflicting pain and suffering its consequences. He had terrified me as a child, but now I have nothing but compassion for the man. LG had always been a head case, but clearly my mother's death destroyed the few strands that connected him to humanity. The day he came to see me at beauty college with those freshly plucked Easter lilies, muddy roots and all, now seemed more pathetic than creepy. Unnerving as it was, his offering had been a tacit kindly gesture, the confused atonement from a fractured individual. As far as I was concerned, his earthly sins were a debt that had been paid in full.

Lutrell and I crisscrossed the country a couple of times with his race car in tow. He was competing at the national level, and that gave us reason to combine sightseeing with his sport. We were having a blast. It was club racing, so off the track, all the competitors were friendly comrades, and by and large, they didn't drink much. You don't want to be hungover in a race car, so my nondrinking was never conspicuous, and I was welcomed into the club with open arms.

But then, in 1999, Lutrell's mother was diagnosed with cancer. She and Lutrell's father had divorced when their children were still young, back in the late 1960s, when she did what a number of women did: she burned her bra and left her marriage, a move that devastated the family but didn't destroy it. I had known Gail since high school, when I was friends with her daughter. Gail was a quintessential Berkeley hippie: she wore paisley and bell-bottoms, she always went barefoot, and she would break out in floaty, lyrical dance moves whenever the mood struck her. She smoked pot, and as a politically active liberal in Marin County, she supported many social-justice causes. She was also a talented artist who marched to the beat of her own drum and appreciated anyone else who did the same. One of my favorite pictures of her is from a trip she took to Thailand. She has a full-faced smile, and I can almost hear her giddy squeal as she holds the heads of two massive snakes that are draped over her shoulders, their thick bodies twined between her legs.

I admired her for her daring and authenticity. When she took me into her heart like a daughter, I welcomed it like a hungry orphan. Treating me like one of her own, I was given gifts for my birthdays and at Christmas. She'd have us over for dinner or take us all out to eat. Family meals were important to her, and she made time for them regularly. I could count on her to contribute her thoughts and feelings about anything I was doing without ever fearing rejection. She was a great mother-in-law to me. She knew how much I loved her son, and that was good enough for her. She never put pressure on me to behave a certain way—or even to have children. I had never felt compelled to be a mother, so I was glad Gail didn't press the subject. She made me feel wholly accepted. In her home, I never feared being turned out or being snubbed. In fact, I can't imagine such a thought ever even occurring to her.

When the cancer struck, it was stronger than she was, and it took her quickly. I loved Gail; she had a big, generous personality and once she was gone, the gaping hole she left in our hearts drew light from every otherwise sunny day. It was as if a tap of enthusiasm had been turned off. Lutrell stopped racing. I quit hairdressing. Although I had been content at my Sonoma hair salon, as an unknown hairdresser in the town, I had to work extra hard to prove myself, and that effort became too draining. I found myself working long hours, trying to be everything to everybody, and I was burning out. It was getting to be where I couldn't muster one iota of concern about the length of my customer's hair, or what product would give them the most body and shine. I was feeling antsy, and Gail's passing gave me just the kick I needed, so I changed professions.

I was ready to do work that wasn't subjective. I had always been good with money, so I figured bookkeeping would be a reasonable second career. Numbers are either right or wrong, and they have nothing to do with taste, style, or status. I took a couple classes at the local junior college, and as soon as they were done, I started picking up temp work. I knew that Lutrell provided a safety net, and I had enough savings that a midlife career change was not all that scary.

Most of my work experience had been in the beauty industry, so I didn't have much of a clue as to how offices functioned. I could do the accounting, but I was a disaster on the telephones, accidentally hanging up on people or transferring their calls to the wrong line. The first time I tried to fax a several-page-long report, I didn't realize that the staples had to be taken out before feeding it through the rollers. I totally jammed the machine and had to get help fixing it.

Eventually I got the hang of my desk job, but before not too long, the irrepressible artist in me started popping out at the seams. I was turning in Excel spreadsheets with fancy fonts, on a diagonal, with colored borders. It took a while before I realized what was happening, but once I did, I had to face facts; I wanted to return to my old job. I called my Sonoma salon, and fortunately, they still had a place for me. I scaled back on the number of hours I would work on any given day, but it didn't take long before I was back in the hairdressing groove. The two-year hiatus I had taken allowed me to purge any and all mid-career doldrums.

Being back behind the stylist's chair was what led to my first writing venture. One day in 2004, I was talking with a customer about the growing popularity of reality TV. I told her how much I couldn't stand the trend. A program called *The Weakest Link* was my prime example. I didn't enjoy the way participants were pitted against each other, shamed and blamed, until the final humiliating moment when one of them would be deemed the most inferior of the group and coldly dismissed from the stage with the phrase, "You are the weakest link. Goodbye." To me, it was gladiatorial. *Survivor* was another popular show that left me cold. Elimination was too sensitive a subject for me. It didn't matter that I had a great life; a part of me still smarted from being kicked off my father's island, so to speak. I told my client that I wanted to see a TV program of inclusion, where every participant was positioned to take advantage of their unique qualifications, and where inspiration and uplift were celebrated. I told her, "I wish I could contribute something to popular culture where the losers were the winners."

Very soon after, a story along those lines took hold of my imagination and wouldn't let go. I found myself waking up from a sound sleep with scenes and dialogue running through my mind. I could see the characters and the narrative arc of the story. It was about a young woman whose husband died suddenly and unexpectedly. Then her ne'er-do-well nephew, who had stolen a valuable set of pearls that had belonged to the protagonist's mother, showed up looking for yet another handout. The two main characters were flawed and hurting, but ultimately, they helped each other heal by heading out on a quest to retrieve the stolen jewelry.

As it happened, a catalogue from a local bookstore arrived in the mail at the same time that my mental obsession with these characters was ramping up. In it were descriptions for several literary events, including a workshop titled, "Is There a Book in You?" For very little money, I could go to the bookstore one night a week, for eight weeks, and figure out what I might do with my losers-are-the-winners story.

At the first session, we all went around and described what books we thought might be in us. At that point I was thinking of my tale as more of a short story than a novel. But when I described it to the class, the facilitator said to me, "That is the most complete description of a novel that I have ever heard from a first-night student."

"Naw," I said, dismissively. But the group chimed in with encouragement, and I was hooked. Before leaving, we all made commitments, declaring the amount of time we would give to our respective projects. I committed to six hours a week, and that was what I did. I stuck with it, and after about a year, I had a first draft. During that year and beyond, I signed up for more writing groups and hired a couple of different editors, and after another three years, my novel, *Pearls My Mother Wore*, was born.

I had written it for two reasons: one, because it wouldn't leave me alone, and two, I figured if I could get it done, meaning written and published, then it would stand as another milestone in my journey. Completion of a full-length writing project would represent additional distance between who I had been in my past as a functionally illiterate kid. I was thrilled when I got the writing done, but trying to get an agent or publisher's attention made crossing the finish line more daunting than I had ever imagined. Looking for endorsements from strangers felt too much like looking for my father. It felt desperate, as if I were asking the literary establishment, "Are you my daddy? Are you my daddy?" I couldn't abide the anticipated rejection. Besides, as an unknown, my chance of being picked up by a mainstream publisher was about one in a gazillion. So, without putting much effort into finding representation, I decided to self-publish.

Once again, I had to face down my finger-wagging internal critic. To that phantom voice I said, "Yes, I know I'm an inexperienced rookie, and I don't exactly know what I'm doing, but I'm going to try anyway." The roaring success and adoring fans in my dreams never materialized, but I birthed that book into the world, and I'm glad I did. It feels good to know that I stayed with the story until it could take on a life of its own. It's a special accomplishment on many levels, and it gives me every reason to hold my head up and stand proud.

It didn't take long after publishing *Pearls My Mother Wore* for my thoughts to circle around to that indefatigable and unresolved subject in my imagination—fathers. I began casting about for a paternal-themed plot, perhaps even one about a girl's search for her lost father. Ideas would come to me, but none of them had the intensity that my first work of fiction possessed. Somehow, every character sketch I came up with seemed unimaginative and incomplete. That's when I began to wonder if it was time for me to reach out, once again, to Mr. Abbott—to work, in effect, on the true-life version of the story. I guessed he would be in his eighties by then, and I hoped that with maturity he might finally respond to an inquiry from me.

I decided that before subjecting his wife to another encounter from yours truly, I would hire a private investigator again to make sure Mr. Abbott was still alive and of sound mind. Showing up at their doorstep would have been cruel and pointless if he had died or was too feeble to talk. I found a PI on the Internet who looked much more appealing than the first guy I had used. Not too young, not too old. He was licensed by the state, and to top it all off, he had a master's degree from UC Berkeley in journalism! He would have the investigative heart and mind that I was after. We spoke on the phone and I told him what I knew. He then asked for a few days to see what he could find out.

It wasn't long before he got back to me with some bombshell information. First, he told me that Gerrick Dean Abbott's wife had died a year and a half before. I knew her name was Margaret, the same as my mother's, so when the PI said, "Margaret has died," I wondered if he had somehow tangled my deceased mother into his research.

"Wait a minute, what? Margaret?"

"Yes. Margaret *Pearl* died in January of 2008."

He had no reason to be pulling my leg, but for a brief moment I wondered if he had googled me and discovered that I had just published *Pearls My Mother Wore*. Not that this made any sense, but I wondered if I was being punked.

"Are you telling me that Margaret Abbott's middle name was Pearl?"

"Yes, I am."

That coincidence sent me into orbit. The odds against the word "pearl" showing up in my life in such incongruent ways seemed astronomical. Instantly I concluded it had to be a sign: my mother, Margaret Jean, and Margaret Pearl, my father's wife, must have been pushing from beyond the grave for the truth to set us all free. I loved the coincidence, but still, I had to have proof. Before I would believe it, I asked, "Can you get me a copy of her death certificate?" He said he could and would. Margaret Pearl was just too rich a detail for me not to include her death record in my rangy family archives.

With the significant information of her passing and her middle name bouncing around in my head, my paid spy moved on to a second bit of information he had discovered. Mr. Abbott, he said, had owned and sold a lot of property, much of which had been off-loaded between the years 2000 and 2004, during a peaking real estate bubble. The PI's voice went heavy with emphasis as he said, "a lot." He said it a couple of times, but I didn't really want to know about Mr. Abbott's financial standing; I didn't want my interest in him and the connection he had to my mother to be clouded by the specter of wealth, so I declined to pursue that detail. It did remind me, however, of Mrs. Abbott's statement so many years prior that Mr. Abbott was afraid I was trying to go after "his children's inheritance." I remember feeling strangely relieved that my father's rejection wasn't just a personal slap; his resistance was also about guarding his ducats, and this new information seemed to affirm that. All the same, I wasn't interested in hearing any more on the money front at that time.

The PI then suggested his next tactic for getting a closer look: he would knock on Gerrick's door under the pretext that he was a reporter doing an article about old bars in the neighborhood. Wow, I loved it. That's got to take nerves of steel. My secret agent was worth every penny of his fee.

A few days went by before he called with a report of his encounter. He explained that when he knocked on Mr. Abbott's door, an elderly woman in a bathrobe answered. When he asked to speak to Mr. Abbott, the woman said that he was unwell and couldn't accept company. My guy told me that it was in the middle of a Sunday afternoon, and he could hear the ball game playing on a television. It was his intuitive guess that the woman was a sister or relative taking care of the old man.

When the PI asked if I wanted him to go back a second time, I told him not to bother. I had learned enough for the time being. I made the assumption that since Mr. Abbott had sold most of his property during a seller's market, he would have had plenty of dough to pay for assisted living if he were seriously infirm. So the fact that he had been home with a ball game blaring led to me to conclude that he was still healthy enough to get one last letter from me. I thanked my secret agent for all he had done and told him I was wildly grateful to him for advancing my cause as much as he had.

That evening I pulled out every document from my mother's strongbox that had Mr. Abbott's name on it. There was no way of knowing who the elderly woman had been, and I was concerned that if she could open Mr. Abbott's front door in a bathrobe, then she may also be in a position to open his mail. I wanted my letter to contain supporting documentation. I didn't want to come across as some sort of Internet scammer making a random claim.

I photocopied my birth certificate, Sean's birth certificate, and the two attorney's letters from 1967. With yellow marking pen, I highlighted every spot where all or part of Mr. Gerrick Dean Abbott's name appeared. Connecting the dots was not exactly straightforward, given all the combinations of Abbott and Ellis I had discovered in the documents before. But I figured that whoever opened my letter would see I had grounds for the inquiry; I wasn't just making up the connection.

After assembling my highlighted photocopies, I attached this letter to my packet:

Dear Gerrick,

I realize that you come to this subject unwillingly, and I apologize, but I'm writing again to ask that you consider meeting me. In July, I turned fifty. I'm not a child. I don't want anything from you but one face-to-face meeting. I wish for nothing more than to be able to put a face and personality onto the blank canvas that represents who you are. Because my mother died when I was sixteen, I was too young to ask her questions about you, a natural curiosity. I knew you existed because of the monthly child support checks you sent. I'm asking with the utmost sincerity that you consider the documents that I have enclosed and help me make sense of them.

I don't think about this everyday, but I have to tell you, when the subject of fathers comes up, and it does, a huge question mark appears for me. Please find it in your heart to sit with me one afternoon so that I can have more than just this vacant canvas.

I've enclosed a self-addressed postcard. Simply name the time and place, and I'll be there.

With earnest interest,
Terry Sue Harms (aka Terry Sue G & Terry Sue Ellis)

I sent the letter and documents by certified mail. A few days later the green return receipt arrived in my mailbox. It was signed "G Abbott." The handwriting was shaky but firm. I didn't think the woman had signed for my packet; the script on the receipt looked masculine. Believing that it was Mr. Abbott's signature, I felt like it was the closest I had ever come to the man himself. I ran my finger over the ink of his handwriting and stared at the postal receipt as if I expected it to speak out loud. I began to wait for my self-addressed post-card to follow, naming a time and place where we could meet. I didn't want to jinx a visit by harboring pessimism, so I stayed sunny and hopeful. With all of my praying might, I wanted him to write back to me.

But as the days passed, so did my optimism. I went from thinking that Mr. Abbott might have an understandable excuse for why he conducted himself the way he did to think-ing he was some kind of jerk. Even if he knew nothing, my letter warranted a response. Any decent human would see that I was pleading. I couldn't understand how or why he would be so heartless and shut off. Compartmentalizing feelings is one thing, but this was like embalming and depositing them into a sealed crypt. Clearly, the man's demons were bigger than mine.

Many of my friends encouraged me to just go knock on his front door; a few of my girlfriends even offered to go with me as support. We amused ourselves at the spectacle we could present if we arrived at his doorstep en masse. We could serenade him, launch a charm campaign, or present him with flowers. All kidding aside, I had to explain that I wasn't interested in giving him another opportunity to reject me. I needed him to buy into the idea of talking with me, and catching him off guard could seriously damage that prospect. And God forbid if pulling off his covers would cause him to become not just hostile but also intensely agitated: the last thing I wanted was to see the man having a coronary right in front of my eyes.

A month went by without getting either a postcard from
Gerrick Dean Abbott or Margaret Pearl's death certificate from my nerves-of-steel spy. I e-mailed the PI to remind
him that I was still waiting, and he responded right away with
an apology and, a few days later, a photocopy of the certificate. I poured over every detail: Margaret Pearl's date of birth,
her level of education, and her maiden name. Further down
the form were boxes that asked for the "Informant's Name . . .
Relationship . . . and Address." I had assumed that Mr. Abbott
would have filled out Margaret Pearl's certificate of death, but
I was wrong: her daughter had.

There it was, typed plain to see, the name and address
of a person who might well be my half sister. What did she
know? Had she overheard anything while growing up? It was
as if a new tiny breadcrumb had been dropped at my feet. It
was a long shot, but by then, I had nothing to lose. If Mr.
Abbott had contacted me, then I wouldn't have felt the need
to expose his daughter to my existence. But before questioning the ethics of getting her involved, I crafted yet another
letter. Upping the ante, I presented myself as if it were an
established fact that she and I were related. On January 10,
2011, this is what I wrote:

Dear Joanne,

*I don't exactly know how to start this introduction, so I'm
going to jump right in. Do you know about me? I introduced myself to your mother about twenty-three years ago.
At that time I also met your brother Gerrick Jr. and his
wife, Sheila. Their daughter, Angela, had just been born.*

Nothing ever came of those meetings; however, I wonder if any of them ever said anything to you? Technically, I'm your half sister. We have the same father. Gerrick is also my brother's father. I'm fifty years old, and he is fifty-three.

If you've never heard about this, I'm sorry to be the first to say anything. I truly do not wish to cause you any upset. My hope is that we may one day soon talk as adults and that you could provide information pertaining to my family history that comes from your side. But I'm also extending myself in this way with the wish that you too would be interested in knowing me.

I've tried to meet Gerrick Abbott four times over the course of my life, but he has silently refused every time. My recent attempt in September was again, sadly, ignored. I've included in this letter a copy of the letter I sent him so that you might understand the nature of my interest. The "documents" I referenced in his letter were my birth certificate, my brother's birth certificate, and two attorney letters from 1967 asking that his child support payments be raised to twenty dollars per week.

I discovered your address from a public Vital Records document concerning your mother's passing. I was saddened to learn of her death; she had been very gracious during an incredibly awkward visit all those years ago. Gerrick wasn't home on that day I mustered the courage to simply knock on their door. The day after my visit, Margaret called and told me he didn't want to meet me. I was hoping in September that he had changed his mind, but clearly not.

As much as I don't understand it, I accept that Gerrick Abbott has his own reasons for staying absent. I simply want you to know I exist and I'm open to meeting you. We *are blood relatives. You may know things about me that I don't even know about myself, things that come from our father's genes. I can understand if you need to take some time to think about this, but please know I would always welcome your contact.*

I included my name, address, phone number, and e-mail. At the post office, I asked for tracking and a return receipt. When the receipt got back to me, it showed that my letter had been forwarded to another address in another state. Somebody with another name had signed for it. I had no idea whose hands my introduction had fallen into. Weeks went by with nothing else showing up. I was crestfallen but not surprised. This journey had included so many dead ends that I was well and truly ready to give up. All I had come to know about Mr. Abbott was that he had engendered both a great deal of loyalty and a strange lack of intimacy. My mother hadn't blown his cover, nor had his wife. The son didn't feel close enough to him to raise the issue, and the daughter was unavailable. Nobody was talking.

Then, on February 7, a month after writing to Joanne, an e-mail arrived in my inbox. She had put her full name in the subject heading, and catching sight of it was an eyepopper. Before opening it, I put my face in my hands and prayed that whatever she had to say wouldn't hurt me. A line from the St. Francis prayer came to mind: "Make me a channel of thy peace." I wasn't looking for a fight. I prayed that her response wouldn't be shaming or defensive. I would not have been keen on any finger wagging or a middle-finger salute in defense of her father.

The e-mail began with an apology for taking so long to get back to me, so that was a comforting start. She said that she had known about Sean and me because when she was fourteen, she had found "some papers." Phew! She said that she had blocked their content from her memory until recently, when she was going through her deceased mother's belongings and came upon them for the second time. She decided then that she would respect her mother and father's lead and say nothing of what she had found. But then my letter arrived, and it stirred up many emotions. She didn't want to upset her father, and they didn't have the kind of open communication that would allow her to intervene on my behalf. She said that she loved him and had always felt his love for her, but they were never close. He was a "workaholic and an alcoholic . . . kindhearted [but] private with his emotions," she explained. But she also said she *was* interested in getting to know me.

I liked her already. She seemed good-willed, diplomatic, and authentic, and I respected what a straight-talker she was. She acknowledged her conflicted feelings without making excuses for them. She was interested in getting to know me, but she also had to respect her father. It would have been easier for her to remain silent, but she was reaching out, and I rejoiced at the effort. She had the paternal embrace, and that set us miles apart, but we were making a start.

In addressing my genealogy and medical concerns, Joanne wrote that Gerrick Abbott was the youngest of eight children. She said that she didn't know those aunts and uncles well since they had all lived in Illinois. She couldn't remember all of their names but gave me the ones she could. The siblings, she believed, had all passed away from cancer. Even Gerrick had had a bout with kidney cancer years before. "They were all heavy smokers and drinkers," she wrote. Next, not knowing my history, she also said this: "Today he is cancer-free and at seventy-nine years old just got out of thirty days inpatient alcohol rehab. Until now he always refused to get help. We were all puzzled as to why he would quit now, but so be it—good for him." She revealed that she too was off alcohol and had been for eleven years. Her brothers had also had "trouble with alcohol." She concluded by telling me that she was married to her high school sweetheart, and they had a thirty-five-year-old daughter and three grandchildren. Her last two sentences were, "Something tells me from the tone of your letter that we have the same temperament. I look forward to hearing from you again. Joanne"

I had hit the mother lode. She wasn't a denier. She was friendly, articulate, sincere, and informative, and I was bowled over. I was ecstatic about the potential for a shift in consciousness within the family and hoped that perhaps Mr. Abbott's alcoholism had played a role in his denial of me. Perhaps he needed to quit in order to feel comfortable about acknowledging that he had a daughter out of wedlock. I called Lutrell into the room to read what she had written. I needed him to assure me that what I was looking at was real—and he did.

Optimism was rekindled. And I have to admit: I was relieved to learn that Joanne had not been given the princess treatment as a child. First of all, I would have found a privileged, imperious attitude hard to take. Secondly, I would have been sick with envy, and it was a comfort to know that I didn't have to be. She had Mr. Abbott in her life, but she wasn't gloating.

I waited until the next morning to send a reply. I wrote "Thank you!" in the subject line and this in the e-mail:

Dear Joanne,

I hope I can adequately express how very grateful I am for your e-mail. It's wonderful to hear from you. We both deserve big pats on the back for our courage. Breaking silence is tough, but it's been my experience that it's worth it. Thank you for taking the risk.

First let me assure you that I don't wish for you to broker a meeting between Gerrick and I. I've made my interest known to him in the softest way I can. I feel it's now up to him to come forward if he'd like. I hope he will, both for my own sake as well as for his, but I'm not pushing.

The alcoholism piece goes a long way in helping me understand his non-reply. In fact, the alcoholism piece is really big. I've been sober for over twenty-three years. My mother died from alcoholism when she was forty-three, and her mother, I believe, died from the disease when she was forty-two. I was lucky, I saw where I was headed, and I changed course. I have a pretty good sense of how delicate life with an alcoholic can be. It would be amazing if Gerrick's rehab sticks, and I truly wish him the best. That you and I share sobriety just knocks me out. Thank you so much for sharing those very personal details with me.

I also appreciate, although it's disconcerting, the medical information. Anything more you can tell me on that subject will be of great value to me: How many aunts, uncles, types of cancer, and age or approximate age when they died? Do you know anything about Gerrick's parents or other generations? Share this with me only if you're comfortable.

I've been happily married for sixteen years. My husband, Lutrell, is my best friend. Although we didn't get married until we were in our thirties, we too have known each other since high school. We don't have any children. I've been a hairdresser for over three decades, and he's a race car mechanic. If you google me, you'll discover that I published a novel titled Pearls My Mother Wore last

February. On its website is a link to my weekly blog that I started last January. There you'll be able to learn a fair amount about me and see several pictures of Lutrell and I. So what do you think? Do we look alike?

I want to be sensitive to the challenging situation I've put you in, so for now, let me just tell you that you've lifted my spirits beyond measure. Thank you for acknowledging me, and I hope this is the beginning of something exciting for both of us.

Over the next nineteen days, Joanne and I swapped twenty e-mails, some of them a couple of pages long. While attempting to maintain adult composure, we were both excited by the prospect of a future together. Our exchanges were filled with exclamation points and smiley faces. As if to make up for lost time, we were quick to reveal personal details about our lives. After saying "my dad" several times, she took a moment to acknowledge that she understood that he was my father too, but she wanted to stick with "my dad" for the time being. Neither of us wanted to hurt the other's feelings or give cause to shut down our fledgling communications. I wrote back to her by saying, "Oh, and thank you for saying that about the 'my dad' thing. He is your dad, and I don't begrudge you that phrase. Somehow I see a difference between the words 'father' and 'dad.' 'Dad' is about the familiar, for-better-or-for-worse, daily interactions you've had with him, and I respect that. 'Father' for me at this point connotes a kind of technical accuracy. He's not just a long-lost friend; he's my father, but he's not my dad."

In March we sent seven e-mails back and forth, in April we sent five, and in May there were four. As our revelations became more and more personal, it became clear that I was at a good place in my life, but Joanne was working through a number of challenges. The level of personal details that she shared in our e-mails deepened and revealed that all was not rosy in her world. She loved her husband and honored her wedding vows to stay together in sickness and in health, but he was a practicing alcoholic, and it tore her up. They were living in two different states while he attempted to get a handle on his drinking. In addition, Joanne was estranged from her thirty-five-year-old daughter and had custody of two of her three grandchildren.

On May 14 we discussed the possibility of meeting at a halfway point for lunch; we lived only four hours apart. But then suddenly our online infatuation came to a screeching halt. Given the level of stress that she was under, it struck me as reasonable that our connection could be tabled for a while. I wasn't going anywhere, and she had repeatedly expressed interest in meeting, so I figured it would happen—all in good time. By August 1, I was the one to break the silence. I attempted to sound light and unconcerned about our precipitous falling-off. The last thing I wanted to do was give her the impression that I was needy or demanding. So I wrote:

> Hi Joanne,
>
> I haven't wanted to make a pest of myself while you've been facing so many challenges, but I am thinking of you and hope you're finding pleasant ways to offset the tough stuff. Have you been able to get in any camping this summer? And are you still planning to see Celine Dion?
>
> Facebook and my blog continue to tell what's been up with me. On Facebook, there is a baby picture of me that I posted. I'm going to be giving less time to the blog for a while. I'm trying to get back into creative writing, so I can't

be spending too much time on the blog. It's all give and take, isn't it?

This summer has been calm and quiet for Lutrell and I. Tomorrow work will finally begin on our big roof repair. After that, I should be getting my new front door. I'll be glad when everything is done. I didn't think we would be taking a vacation this year because of the construction expenses, but it turns out that we are. We've planned to go up the coast for several days at the end of September. First we will spend a couple of nights at the Little River Inn just south of Mendocino, then a couple of nights in Garber-ville at the Benbow Inn, and then four nights at Redwood National Park. If the weather cooperates, it should be absolutely lovely for hiking and biking, our favorite! If we get early rains, I guess I have plenty of reading to do. Who knows, maybe I'll bring my laptop and actually get in some writing of my own as well. Have you been to any of these areas? I've been collecting recommendations of places to see along the way.

Until next time, wishing you the best,
Terry

She wrote back the next day, but her tone was different—distant. The sentence that cut me to the quick was, "I think of you often and feel I'm doing you a disservice by not being more attentive to developing our relationship." It was clear she was trying to let me down easy, but the whole tenor of the e-mail struck a false note for me. It sounded like the classic "It's not you, it's me" breakup line. She was in the driver's seat, but I felt that if we couldn't meet as equals, then I didn't want to meet at all. We had gone as far as we could, and it was time to back off.

That was our last e-mail, and it's been years since then.

As quickly as we started, that's how quickly we stopped. It hurt—a lot—partly because it felt like my last chance to enlist any help in getting to Mr. Abbott. I was also disappointed because Joanne and I had been developing a genuinely nice relationship, mindful of being honest while at the same time not laying heavy trips on each other. But I soon came to realize that perhaps it was best for both of us to take a breather. If we had become truly close, then it would have been increasingly difficult to ignore Gerrick Abbott, which we had made a point of doing in our e-mails. Pressure would have mounted for her to step in and challenge her father on the subject of Sean and Terry Ellis, and as was the case with Junior, she had already told me she and her "dad" weren't close, so she probably wouldn't be able to do that. And how could we continue with that elephant still in the room?

But I had received plenty of worthwhile tidbits from Joanne Abbott, so I was grateful for our fleeting encounter. Also, in hindsight, I came to feel a bit guilty about my own motives in pursuing our relationship. I had to admit to myself that I had been driven in large part by my desire to get to the bottom of my father question. I invented an air of friendly curiosity, but in truth, I was hungrily scouring her every word for information I could use. And my intention was to keep that tap flowing for as long as I could. The fact of the matter is that we had never been equals, and we never would be as long as Mr. Gerrick Dean Abbott, whoever he was, stayed in hiding. Despite our split, we continue to be "friends" on Facebook, although we never commented on each other's posts.

Two years after communication with Joanne Abbott had dried up, I found myself consumed with the idea of Father's Day. I was shopping for a card for my father-in-law, and every one of them made me angrier and angrier. "You've always been there for me, Dad." "You're my best friend, Dad." "I owe it all to you, Dad." I needed to repeat a calming mantra in order to get through the purchase: deep cleansing breaths, deep cleansing breaths. Even though I was shopping for Lutrell's dad, I was thinking about my own father and wondering, yet again, what the hell had gone on. The unfairness of his disappearance was insufferable. I was tormented by the fact that when a child goes missing, it's headline news, but when a parent goes missing, it hardly generates a second thought. It's, "Those things happen," "Too bad," "Boys will be boys." At best I might hear, "That's a shame." But what I wanted was a communal outcry, a dogged search team, friends, family, and perfect strangers working day and night to find him—or at least to generate some answers.

I couldn't shake my frustration and despair, so at the end of that Father's Day Sunday, I turned to my mother's strongbox to review her enigmatic documents once again. I had been in possession of the strongbox ever since I snatched it out of LG's house of horrors almost four decades earlier. And over the years, I had searched its contents over and over for clues. I held documents up to the light to see if there were any watermarks; I took a magnifying glass to them, like a forensic examiner; I called on my higher power to give me clues. But when nothing came of it, I had to accept that I didn't get to have the final word, no matter how much I wanted it. But then, on that particular Father's Day, I made a fresh observation.

Initially I doubted myself and didn't want to get too excited. But for the first time in all those years of combing through the strongbox, a different interpretation of a key piece of evidence jumped out at me. It was in the subject heading of the two attorney letters where it read, "Ellis vs. Abbott." I had always assumed that was just the legal way to reference "my client vs. your client." The correspondences had been between the two attorneys. But for some reason, this time it occurred to me that perhaps the heading was the title of a court case. I wondered if Ellis vs. Abbott had actually been a trial with a verdict, in which case there would be a public record of the proceedings, and the mysterious antagonists in my life might be identified. The next morning, I started a new search to see if there was any wind for this new tack.

Because I had lived in Alameda County in 1967, I typed "Alameda County Court Records" into my computer search engine. The first hit to pop up was a link to the superior court records website. At the top of the page, I read, "Most case records are available to the public and may be viewed and copied at most court locations throughout Alameda County." That told me that I didn't have to be covert, or prove who I was or why I was interested in viewing the files, and that was a tremendous relief.

I also saw on the website, "Individuals may research court records in person at no cost." Another comfort. I didn't have to pay a lawyer to get what they had. Still, a grain of skepticism tempered my confidence. I would be dealing with a government bureaucracy, so missing, mysteriously disappeared, or careless misfilings were all a possibility. But I crossed my fingers and went on.

The website had a list of phone numbers for the different records units—civil, criminal, family law, juvenile, probate, or adoption—so I picked family law. But that department couldn't help me, and they directed me to the unit for civil court. My heart was knocking against my chest as I made the call. I had felt this excitement before without any results, so I was prepared to be disappointed again.

The woman who answered the phone was pleasant and professional. I told her that I was looking for a possible court case between my biological parents, that it may or may not have occurred in California, and that it could have been any time between 1957 and 1967. I told her I had two letters between attorneys dated 1967 that both referred to "Ellis vs. Abbott," but it wasn't clear what those names represented. She asked me to spell both names. I could hear her rapid keystrokes as she entered my information into a computer.

When she came back with an actual case number, I wanted to hug her through the phone. I forced myself to calm down long enough to hear that the file was a civil case, "not confidential," but "index only." I didn't know what any of that meant, so she explained that I would have to go to the courthouse in Oakland to view the file on microfiche. She gave me the address and phone number and suggested that I call ahead to check on their hours.

Holy mother of God, I had something! I didn't know what in the world would be in the court transcript, but I knew I had to get it. I made immediate arrangements to go the next morning. While the hours passed, I imagined any number of ghastly scenarios that could thwart me once again: everything from dropping dead of a heart attack to a courthouse firebomb. My imagination was all over the place. The next morning's bumper-to-bumper traffic felt like a cruel cosmic joke. And when I missed the freeway exit and got lost in a labyrinth of city streets, it only added to the mythic quality of my quest.

The twelve-story art deco courthouse is situated right next to shimmering Lake Merritt. I had been there before. In fact, it was at the registrar of voters office within the building that I, some thirty-three years earlier, had found the first tidbits of information about Gerrick Abbott: his new address and the possibility that he had his wife and my mother both pregnant at the same time. Although the lake is named after a Dr. Merritt, an early resident of the area, I always hear it as Lake Merit, as in worthiness of a cause. So I took the building's location as an encouraging portent. Satisfaction had been so elusive over the years, but at the shore of my Lake Worthiness, I was really starting to hope.

The department of records management was across the street from the grand courthouse. I went inside and told an armed guard I was looking for room 16, and he directed me to the basement. As I descended to the windowless bowels of the building, the quiet, narrow staircase made me slightly claustrophobic. Once in the basement, the walls were bare, and the long, beige corridor was lit by—what else?—florescent lights. It was Kafkaesque.

Inside room 16, the paint scheme shifted from beige to pumpkin orange, and a surprisingly chipper clerk asked if I needed any help. He was nothing like the worker-drone I was expecting from the drabness of the decor. He typed in the case number I'd handed him and stepped away from the window. When he came back, he ushered me to a glassed-in room where the microfiche readers were. He flicked on the light and loaded the reel of film that contained my Ellis vs. Abbott file. After a brief tutorial on how to operate the antiquated equipment, he left me to my research. With the door closed, the small room was soundproof, and I was quickly oblivious to the comings and goings of the outer office. After what seemed like an eternity of scrolling, my exact file number appeared. I took a deep breath and told myself that I was prepared for anything.

I froze at the blizzard of words that swirled before my eyes. Focus, I had to focus. Microfiche is a film negative, so the pages are dark and the writing is light, white text on a black background. I could look at the microfilm, but I couldn't read it. The more I tried to concentrate, the more panicky I became. I understood what was happening to me—nothing impedes my ability to pick sentences off a page like having to read on demand. And these particular words might just solve the mystery that had plagued me for over fifty years, so you can imagine the pressure. I gave myself a few additional minutes to gather my thoughts and let my brain adjust. I wasn't going to be able to skim or speed-read. I needed to settle down. I was going to read every word and not go on until I was certain that I understood what I had just finished. It called for the same discipline I had practiced when I first started reading books.

Beginning at the top left of the first page, I saw the address block for my mother's attorneys:

HOLMDAHL & FLETCHER
Attorneys at Law
1624 Franklin Street
Oakland 12, California
TEmplebar 6-0650

I immediately recognized the name Holmdahl. John Holmdahl had drafted my mother's last will and testament. He had been a California state senator from 1958 until 1982, an Oakland city councilman, and an appellate court judge until retiring. I don't know how my mother came to have

John Holmdahl as her legal representative, but there he was, and I was impressed.

Opposite the attorney's address was the imprint of a rubber stamp:

FILED
1960 SEPTEMBER 22, PM 4:18
SUMMONS ISSUED

That date would have been the day after my mother's twenty-seventh birthday. I would have been two months old. That stamp located these proceedings seven years prior to my two Ellis vs. Abbott letters. That meant that Ellis vs. Abbott had been going on, essentially, since the time I was born.

Along the left-hand margin, every line of official text was numbered. On line 10, my mother was listed with her first-marriage name, Margaret Jean Ellis, as "Plaintiff." On line 13, Gerrick Dean Abbott was listed as "Defendant." The text of line 12 read in all capital letters:

COMPLAINT TO ESTABLISH PATERNITY OF MINOR CHILDREN AND TO PROVIDE SUPPORT

"Minor children," plural, so this wasn't just about Sean's father. This was about Sean and me, since my brother Gordon had never been an issue. He knew who his father was, Eugene Ellis.

My mother's allegations were numbered with Roman numerals. The first one established that she was a resident of the county and lived in the state of California. Five additional claims and petitions followed:

II   Plaintiff is the mother of minor children Sean Avery Ellis, age 3 years, born June 11, 1957, and of Terry Sue Ellis, age 2 months, born July 24, 1960

III Defendant is the father of said minor children

IV Plaintiff does not have sufficient funds with which to support and maintain said children; Defendant has sufficient funds and income with which to pay a reasonable sum for the support of said minor children

V That Plaintiff does not have sufficient funds with which to pay fees to her attorneys for services rendered and to be rendered in behalf of said minor children in this action or to pay Court costs herein; that Defendant is able-bodied, capable of earning a substantial income, and financially able to pay reasonable amounts for each and all the foregoing items;

VI Plaintiff does not have sufficient funds wherewith to pay hospital and doctor bills which were incurred in the connection with the birth of each of said children; that said expenses, exclusive of the payments resulting from insurance coverage, are $125.00 for medical expense in connection with the birth of Sean and $75.00 medical expense and $104.00 hospital expense in connection with the birth of Terry

WHEREFORE, Plaintiff prays judgment as follows:

1. That Defendant be declared to be the father of said minor children;

2. That Defendant be ordered to pay a reasonable sum of money per month for the support of said children;

3. That Defendant be ordered to pay a reasonable sum of money for the medical and hospital expenses attendant upon the birth of said children;

4. That Defendant be required to pay a reasonable sum of money for the cost of this action and for Plaintiff's attorneys' fees; and

5. For such other and further relief as to the Court may seem just and proper.

There it was, her assertions laid out in clear, straightforward language. Margaret Jean Ellis may have been a penniless, unwed mother of three, but she wasn't going to be shamed into silence. Sean and I weren't mistakes, bastards, or dirty little secrets. She contended that we were Gerrick Dean Abbott's two children, and if what she claimed was true, Mr. Abbott was not going to get away with abdicating all responsibility for us.

Half of the allegations had to do with money. Financial insecurity had been a constant in our lives, and it came as no surprise to have it identified here in the summons. The dollar amounts sounded miniscule, but they wouldn't have been in 1960. Inside my mother's strongbox was a pay stub of hers, dated March 20, 1960. After forty hours of work, her take-home pay was $72.69. Food, housing, furniture, general health care, childcare, transportation, and clothing would have been crushing on that salary; add in legal fees and hospital bills, and some part of her must have felt destitute. She needed to establish who the father of her two youngest children was and have him share in the financial burdens of their care.

The next document to appear on the microfilm was an official income-and-expense questionnaire. At the top of the form was a line to identify whether it was "Husband or Wife" who was answering the money questions. Neither had been circled; instead, "Mother" had to be typed in. She listed her only asset as household furnishings valued at $100. There were no business assets, no bank accounts, no real estate, stocks, or bonds. Under the "Motor Vehicles" category, for value, the word "Negligible" was written. As for necessary monthly expenses for her two minor children in the paternity suit, she listed: $20 for clothes, $10 for doctors and dentists, $60 for food, $40 for incidentals, $90 for childcare, $45 for rent, and $10 for utilities: $275 total. She stated that her gross monthly income was $350. That meant that after paying $275 for Sean and me, she had an unsustainable $75 left over to cover Gordon and herself per month. Eugene Ellis had never paid child support for Gordon, and in my mother's strongbox were numerous collection letters addressed to him, illuminating his fiscal wreckage. Ellis was a dead end, but Abbott must have been worth going after. On the microfiche questionnaire, my mother requested $55 per month per child for support. That was sounding more than fair, as it was less than half her total estimated expenditures. She also requested $250 in legal fees, $30 in court costs, plus payment of her medical and hospital bills that were connected to Sean's and my births.

The next page of microfilm was a "Proof of Service" form that identified October 2, 1960 as the day Gerrick Dean Abbott was served my mother's complaint and summons. In addition to my mother's filings, a general summons from the State of California, dated October 18, was also served. It read in part:

THE PEOPLE OF THE STATE OF CALIFORNIA

To the above named Defendant(s):

You are hereby directed to appear and answer the complaint of the above named Plaintiff(s) filed in the above entitled court in the above entitled action brought against you in said court within TEN days after the service on you of this summons . . .

The order went on to declare that if Gerrick Dean Abbott failed to do so, then Margaret Jean Ellis would be awarded her monetary demands, with rights to further court actions. And it described the granting of custody to my mother, "with rights of reasonable visitation to defendant."

The court date was set for November 1.

On October 27, one day before the ten-day deadline for his response, Gerrick Dean Abbott formally submitted three documents of his own. The first was his financial questionnaire. His fiscal accounts were an improvement over my mother's, but he wasn't a rich man. His average net earnings were reported as $105 weekly. He had no private business assets, no funds in bank accounts, and no stock or bond investments. He had $150 worth of household furnishings, a 1953 Buick worth $150, and $1,000 in real estate equity. His monthly expenses added up to $477, and he stated that he had $1,000 in debts.

The second submission was called a DECLARATION IN OPPOSITION TO DECLARATION FILED HERE IN BY MARGARET JEAN ELLIS.

In it, Mr. Abbott's attorney, Charles R. Way, had this to say: " . . . the complaint states insufficient facts to state a cause of action . . ." This sounded like he was saying: prove it. In other words, just because Margaret claimed that Abbott was the father of her two youngest children didn't mean that he was.

Mr. Abbott also asserted, through his lawyer, that he " . . . is married to a woman other than plaintiff and has three minor children by said marriage . . ."

The third submission was a DEMURRER TO COMPLAINT, which laid out Abbott's reasons why this paternity suit was not justified. One being that my mother couldn't prove that he was the father, and two, she couldn't prove that Eugene Ellis, her ex-husband, didn't father *all* of her children.

Well, well, well. I had prepared for anything, but this was odd. Until I was fifteen years old, those monthly $90 checks had arrived in our mailbox with Mr. Abbott's return address on the outside of the envelopes. So his pointing to Eugene Ellis had my head spinning. Could his assertion be true? The checks stopped arriving just before Sean turned eighteen and I was fifteen. Had I mistaken the significance of those stopped checks? Could it be that my mother had two children from her first marriage, and the pittance of child support was deemed to be for me alone? Or could my mother have had Gordon with Ellis, Sean with Abbott, and me with some third unnamed man? Or was Mr. Abbott's postulation nothing more than a red herring? I had to keep reading.

In something called a **REQUEST STIPULATION AND ORDER FOR TRANSFER**, the trial was postponed and moved, but in the meantime, it was ordered that both parties, and the children named in the complaint, take blood tests—paid for by the defendant—by December 1. Furthermore, the court stipulated that if it was established that my mother was meritorious in her claims, then Gerrick Dean Abbott would be required to pay $250 for my mother's legal fees on a schedule of $50 per month; he would have to pay her court costs and medical bills, and it was determined that he would pay $52.50 per child per month in child support. That was not quite the $55 per month per child my mother had been asking for, but it still didn't explain the $90 figure she was receiving in 1975.

The next pages, filed on November 16, 1960, were Gerrick Dean Abbott's deposition taken by my mother's attorneys, Holmdahl and Fletcher. With the outcome of the blood tests still pending, and in the company of his own lawyer, Charles R. Way, Mr. Abbott replied again and again to my mother's allegations with two phrases: "denies each and every allegation" and "he has no information or belief on the subject."

His deposition concluded with an assertion that he was not financially able to pay Holmdahl and Fletcher's attorney fees, and that it was his belief that my mother was married to Eugene Ellis at the time Sean Avery Ellis was conceived.

The next page to scroll onto the screen appeared very different from all the preceding pages. It was dated December 5, 1960, and it was a minute-by-minute courtroom transcript for the case titled Ellis vs. Abbott. At the top of the page were the names of four presiding officials, plus Holmdahl, Fletcher, Way, and Abbott—a room of eight men and my twenty-seven-year-old mother.

Blow by blow, the proceedings read as follows:

Action (Non-Jury) assigned from Dept. One.

From 10:20 a.m. to 10:29 a.m. the Court and respective counsel confer in chambers.

At 10:30 parties and counsel are present in the courtroom and Margaret Jean Ellis is sworn and examined in her own behalf as plaintiff.

Defendant now admits being the father of Terry Sue Ellis. Issue now is whether defendant is the father of Sean Avery Ellis.

A few more routine proceedings were documented as cards and letters to my mother from Gerrick Abbott were admitted into evidence. Unfortunately, that corroborating ephemera was not included in the microfiche file. I would have loved to see those personal correspondences between my parents. Clearly, my mother believed they proved my father's involvement. I like to think they were love letters to her and birthday cards to his son, but that's my fantasy. The "trial" then concluded with this:

> At 11:10 a.m. Gerrick Dean Abbott is sworn and examined as an adverse witness for plaintiff.

> At 11:52 a.m. both sides rest.

> At 11:53 a.m. matter submitted, Court announces its decision to wit: first that, defendant is adjudged to be the father of Terry Sue Ellis; secondly that defendant is adjudged to be the father of Sean Avery Ellis.

That was it. Within less than an hour, the determination was made that Mr. Gerrick Dean Abbott was both Sean's and my father.

You'd think after all the time that I had search for this answer, I would have fallen down in a dead faint at the news. Instead, I was completely numb. The dry, legalese facts of the matter left me drained of any dramatic response, as if my emotions had been given a shot of novocaine. In that sound-proofed little microfiche room, with my back to the main office, I didn't feel like crying, or shaking my fist, or hitting a wall. I think I was experiencing the first stage of grief: denial. Not that I didn't believe what had just been laid out; I was denying that it affected me. The many forms of Gerrick Dean Abbott that I had imagined over the years ceased to exist then and there. My fantasy father was gone, and in his place was Defendant Gerrick Dean Abbott, my biological progenitor. The full impact of that shift, the death of my illusion, was yet to come. In the moment, I thought I was fine.

The court transcript also contained its multifaceted decision: that Gerrick Dean Abbott had to reimburse my mother $90.00 on my account and $140.10 on account of Sean for hospital expenses incurred during our births, as well as $40.00 for Dr. T. Spindler and $49.16 for Eden Hospital; that Abbott had to pay a total of $156.50 to my mother's lawyers, and that he would be responsible for $8.00 per week of child support for each child. And in a separate procedural submission from Holmdahl and Fletcher, which basically reiterated the court's findings, Abbott was ordered to pay any future hospital, medical, and dental expenses that Sean and I would require.

That was a blow. Growing up, I had been under the impression that we couldn't afford medical care, so I learned to avoid doctors and dentists as much as possible. When I had that impetigo, I had to rely on the neighbor lady taking pity on me and bringing me to her own doctor. When I needed dental work, I was taken to a dental college in San Francisco, where the smallest filling took three hours to fill. The fillings cost only three dollars, but I have jaw troubles to this day as a result of holding my mouth open for hours on end while student dentists practiced on me. The day I hobbled home after cutting my bare foot on a piece of glass, my mother's reaction was not one of concern; it was resentment: "Goddamn it! What have you done now?" There was no money to pay a doctor to fix me, but she couldn't staunch the bleeding, so we had to go to the emergency room. Eight stitches and a pair of crutches later, my mother was livid.

And this neglect had lasting repercussions, which still require a steady amount of positive self-talk. As an adult, I've had to train myself to take my health seriously and spend the money when needed. When I've been unwell, I've had to assure myself that I will be taken care of and that it's okay to ask for help.

But the real kicker was what I read in a paragraph further down the screen:

IT IS FURTHER ORDERED, ADJUDGED, AND DECREED that
Plaintiff is entitled to the sole custody of said children and
that Defendant is not entitled to said custody nor to any
rights of visitation in connection with said children.

With the strike of a gavel, my father had been eliminated
from my life. I was just a few months old, a baby. What could
I say? "Your Honor, I object!" Why was this the best course of
action? The best for whom? In an instant, Mr. Abbott was not
only given permission to walk away, he was ordered to do so,
Sean and I be damned.

The final microfilm documents to surface were the court
proceedings that predated the two Ellis vs. Abbott letters
that had mystified me from the time I first discovered them.
This last proceeding came six years later. In June of 1966, my
mother returned to the judicial system to seek an increase
in her support payments. Her appeal for a modification sites
changing conditions and circumstances:

a. The mere passage of time has brought attendant infla-
tion and increased costs of living; b. the ages of the children
are such that they are now requiring considerably larger
amounts to support; plaintiff has heretofore and until recent
months been employed through the intervening period of
time; plaintiff has remarried and has another child and is
unable to return to work.

Gerrick countered with a total dismissal of the request:

The plaintiff herein is capable of obtaining good employment, and I feel that she should share in the support of the
children of whom I was adjudged to be the father.

I don't think Mr. Abbott was clear on the concepts of
sharing and support. In what sounded like completely circular

reasoning, he also had the audacity to swear off financial responsibility by claiming ignorance of his financial affairs:

That following said judgment of paternity and for support I turned over all of my financial affairs to my wife and I am not too familiar with my family expenses.

He must have believed there was a thread of logic in his statements, but I felt my brain freak out in trying to follow it. It was almost like I was experiencing a bad acid trip. Was he saying that my mother wasn't doing enough? Did he see *himself* as the victim? Why would the fact that his wife handled his checkbook absolve him of responsibility for his children? His statements were followed by one from his wife. She pointed out that she and her husband had three children and that she had always maintained her job as a bookkeeper, a thinly veiled dig at my mother and her four children. The implication was that if she could take care of three children, then why couldn't my mother manage with just one more? Apples to apples, right? Mrs. Abbott itemized her family's income and expenses to illustrate that Gerrick's income fell short of their expenses. The deficit, she explained, was covered by her bookkeeping income and from a rental property they owned. She declared under penalty of perjury that what she claimed was true and correct, and then she signed the document.

That was the end of the complete file.

I didn't know what to make of all I had read. My big question, "Was Gerrick Dean Abbott my biological father?" had been answered. But nothing in the file helped me figure out what to do with that knowledge. It was as though I was looking at a patch of fur while unaware that it was attached to a giant gorilla.

I returned to the clerk and asked if I could get a paper

copy of the complete file. He said yes, but that it would be of poor quality and would cost fifty cents per page. If he had said five dollars a page, I would have paid it, and as for the quality, I'd take whatever I could get.

Again, irrational fears of disaster surfaced, and I started imagining hot light bulbs melting my film. I could just picture the stricken young clerk holding out a glob of unreadable plastic ooze after the microfiche machine malfunctioned. Over all of the proceeding years, I had been stymied so many times that I hesitated to trust that those vital records, my proof, would not somehow be lost forever. My nerves were fraught at that point, and the whole scene was beginning to feel absurd. When the clerk called over a supervisor to help him with the file conversion, my ears perked up. When I heard him say, from around the corner, "Why does it keep disappearing like that?" I had to sit down. I remember thinking, "God's will be done. Let go, and let God."

I don't think I took another breath until that clerk was back in front of me with a sheaf of pages and this innocuous request: "Alrighty then, that will be eighteen dollars, ma'am."

e knew! All the years I spent in the dark, and he knew. I began to seethe. When I thought about how I had pussy-footed around this man, soft-pedaling my every inquiry, never knowing whether he was or wasn't my father, I wanted to spit. No matter how I tried to reframe his actions, there was no way I could make them acceptable. For the next several days, sentences from the Ellis vs. Abbott case would come back to me—and I would be stinking mad. I felt like a hissing caul-dron, always on the verge of spilling over. My husband was unsure how to handle me, but to his credit, he went the loving route. More than usual, he'd tell me he loved me, that he was proud of me, and that I was beautiful. For no apparent reason, he would embrace me in a hug and hold on until he could feel my body relax into his. He'd tell me that Abbott didn't know what he was missing.

For about a week, I stewed in the muck. Since the whole family refused to own up, I was left holding the burden of their unfinished business. Was the assumption that what I didn't know wouldn't hurt me? That my ignorance was bliss? If so, they were wrong. I was the one who had to go around explaining why I didn't have a father, or even much of an idea of who he was. I could either lie about him or tell an unflat-tering truth about having a father who wanted nothing to do with me. Through no fault of my own, I was imprinted with a lesser status; I was illegitimate. Polite people wouldn't say it, but the rude ones did: I was the bastard daughter of a stranger.

It felt like everyone involved in this sorry drama had for-gotten about me in one way or another. With the clap of a gavel, the judge and lawyers all got to go home and never think about me again. With her last guzzle of booze, my mother forgot about me. With a wife to do his bidding, my father forgot about me. And I alone felt the sting of my father's neglect. If he had cut off my arm, there's no way he would have been able to get away with his disappearing act. But because his severance left no visible marks, he was allowed to walk free. If babies were able to speak, then child abandonment would be a federal crime.

As I wrestled with the new information I had received from the court case, I tried to make sense of the era in which it had occurred. Women's rights at the time of my birth were abysmal. The Food and Drug Administration had only just approved the sale of birth control pills. Before I was born and even afterwards in some states, the mere mention of contraception was illegal. So-called "Chastity Laws" and the Comstock Act prohibited sending birth control literature and devices in the mail. Such items and information were deemed obscene and made a federal crime punishable by fines and imprisonment. Although Margaret Sanger had embarked on a campaign to reform the reproductive rights of women in 1915, it wasn't until 1957, a mere three years before I was conceived, the year Sean and Gerrick Jr. were born, that the Comstock Law was terminated. Still, a notion persisted that birth control was indecent, and it wasn't until 1965 that the Supreme Court established the right of married couples to practice contraception. Terminating an unwanted pregnancy, *for any reason*, was illegal until 1973. And it wasn't until 1993 that all fifty states had laws to protect women against rape in marriage. (Until then, men had the "marital exception" to rape their wives.) My mother had been dead for three years when the Pregnancy Discrimination Act was finally passed; before that, a woman could be fired from her job just for getting pregnant. No wonder my family drama revolved around a woman, my mother, not living a traditionally acceptable life. My mother staggered under the social and moral burdens of those times far more than my father ever did.

And that's just the procreation side of it. There were many other ways in which the deck was stacked against women like my mother such as: up until 1974, when the Senate passed the Equal Credit Opportunity Act, women could be denied credit cards or home and business loans because of their gender. It's unlikely that my mother ever thought about starting a business, but a) you never know, and b) not being able to get a credit card or a home loan certainly didn't help a woman establish any kind of financial independence.

And while all of that was going on, my father and his wife were amassing a real estate fortune! His daughter, my half sister Joanne, had told me during our e-mailing that her dad owned a considerable number of rental properties: apartment complexes in Reno, Nevada, and a 180-unit apartment building in Modesto, California. (I never told her that my private detective had tipped me off to the sizable California properties that Gerrick Abbott held and had sold during the real estate boom.)

My friends were fascinated to hear about what I had learned, but when my vehemence burst forth as from the head of Medusa, even the ones who knew me best would show alarm. More than once I heard, "I've never seen you like this." I, too, was a bit worried about my volatile emotions. Whoever said that resentment was the number one killer of alcoholics was truly onto something. But I was determined not to let this pathetic situation get the better of me—and certainly not to let it drive me back to drinking. At the same time, I wasn't going to just roll over. I was mad as hell and couldn't just, poof, "Let it go."

I did manage to stay sober, even though my anger and my search for answers never abated. There was no denying that my father had been an epic failure, but I couldn't stop mulling over various possible explanations for his behavior. Joanne had told me that Gerrick had been hearing-impaired since childhood, and that he had been honorably discharged from the army because of it. She also said that he dropped out of school in the ninth grade, and when he was thirteen or fourteen, his father kicked him out of the house. It seemed plausible that a person who could not hear the world and who had been rejected by his father might have a hard time bonding with people. Who knows?

I had two hairdressing customers that I could talk with openly about my feelings, a retired couple named Stan and Leva Metz. Leva had been a social worker, and Stan had been a psychiatrist for the criminally insane at Napa State Hospital—careers that seemed designed to engender insight and compassion (or at least attract people who already had those qualities). Stan had a full head of silver hair, bushy white eyebrows, and a beard to rival Santa's. He was a gentle giant, standing over six feet tall and weighing well over two hundred pounds. Leveling his limpid eyes at me, he would ask:

"Terry, what is it that you want from this man?"

"I want to hear his side of the story. I want to know who he is and what he was thinking."

Stan laughed a jolly belly laugh, and when it settled, he said, "Terry, do you honestly believe he knows what he's thinking?" And at that, we both laughed.

After a pause for thought, he then asked, "What are you afraid of?"

"I'm afraid he's going to be a self-satisfied prig, a woman-hater. I'm afraid he'll be dismissive of his conduct and insulting towards my mother. I'm afraid he's going to be mean-spirited, an old man who would rather die than face the truth."

"Terry, what do you say we go to his house together? I don't have to say a word. We can knock on his door and ask to talk. He will see what a fine young woman you have turned out to be. I think you should give him a chance."

"Stan, I've given him four chances. I can't give him yet another opportunity to shut the door in my face, literally *and* figuratively. But thank you. You're the best, Stan."

We looked at each other in the mirror. His face was slightly pained, but when our eyes met, he softened and then gave me a loving and accepting smile.

"Let's talk about something else," I suggested.

Now, just because I refused his help didn't mean that I didn't appreciate his offer or that the matter had been settled; I hadn't given up my ruminations of retribution. It moved me immeasurably that Stan was concerned enough about me to not just talk about my issues, but to actually volunteer to meet the man whom I'd described in such vicious terms. But in my thoughts, I just knew I couldn't walk the same path that had led to failure so many times before.

So instead of taking Stan up on his offer, I decided that if Gerrick Dean Abbott wouldn't meet with me personally, then he would have to meet me in a court of law. I had learned that there was no statute of limitations on collecting child support. Abbott owed my mother three years' worth of payments. He had stopped sending checks when I was fifteen, but they should have continued until I was eighteen. I began looking for an attorney who could help me collect what was owed to us. My mother had fought for me—at least in this respect—and I was going to finish the job. It didn't even matter that a good lawyer would probably charge more than any back pay of child support I might be able to collect on my mother's behalf; I didn't care. I wanted to see his face. I wanted him to know that I knew what he had done. I wanted the record to reflect his neglect, and I wanted to see him publicly outed for being a deadbeat dad.

Somewhere between my thinking and acting, however, I realized that revenge wasn't what I wanted after all. I didn't want Mr. Abbott's money, his accolades, or his friendship. What I was after more than anything was a sincere apology. I wanted him to say, of his own volition, "I'm sorry. I'm sorry that my poor decisions affected your life. When it comes to the father piece, I blew it, and I am so sorry."

Still, I knew how unlikely that was. I had been unable to get anything from him for so many years; why would it change now? No courtroom judge would be able to demand the heartfelt apology and recognition of harm done that I was looking for. I decided not to proceed with a lawsuit as I was realizing that I simply had to let him go. I had to release the dream of an *us*, as loving father and daughter. I had to find other ways to get over my profound disappointment.

One thing that helped me along that path was the realization that Gerrick Dean Abbot's refusal to recognize me as his daughter had to have been only part of a much bigger failure of character. I didn't know the details of what he had been through in his life, but his denial of two of his own children was enough to tell me that he was deeply flawed—so much so that I no longer wanted to invite him into my world. If the man couldn't recognize his own loss, and the drain on his life that came from turning his back on his own creation, then what could he possibly have to offer me? He had to come around to viewing fatherhood and me in a whole different light. If that could happen, then I would welcome the shift, but in the meantime, I knew as much of my biological father as I wanted to know. It would be a meeting initiated by his free will or zilch.

o here's the stinger: four years went by during which I worked hard on acceptance, on letting go, and on finding a place in my heart for forgiveness—only to find out that Gerrick Dean Abbott Sr. had been dead that whole time. He had died just ten days after I had discovered my mother's paternity suit, right when I was at the height of my fury and preparing to drag him into court.

This information came to me in the hair salon. I was with a client who was an Internet sleuth and had found fascinating details about her own deceased father and ancestors. She was well aware of my paternity saga and casually asked my father's name. She clicked away on her computer tablet as I snipped and styled her hair. She drilled down a few pages and then said, "Ah, oh. He died four years ago."

I had enough presence of mind to stop cutting and hang my head for a moment to absorb the impact of that irreversible fact. However hard I had tried to let go and forgive this man over the past four years, it was clear that I had also been holding out hope that, one day, against the odds, he would come clean with me. But now there was no doubt that his answer to me was a definitive no: my father would never acknowledge me as his daughter.

That hairdressing client is also a dear friend, and I knew she wouldn't be offended when I responded, "Motherfucker." She could see that the color had drained from my face, and she repeatedly asked if I was okay. I assured her that I was, but honestly, I was in shock. I closed up the salon and went home, all my movements as if on autopilot. When I told Lutrell the news, it was as if I were relaying some inconsequential detail of the day, as if I were telling him that I had just put gas in the car. It was only when he stopped what he was doing and came to me that I got a sense of just how numb I had gone. Within his embrace, I stood not knowing what to say or do.

At first I was incredulous. Why hadn't Joanne, my half sister, let me know? We had stopped e-mailing each other two years before our father died, but not on unpleasant terms. She was well aware of my desire for answers from him. She could have gotten word to me, if not immediately, at least at some point since then. I had kept our Facebook connection open specifically to see if a post of hers would one day announce his passing and the end of my questing. The evening I found out about Gerrick's death, I searched four years of Joanne's Facebook posts to see if I had missed it, but nothing turned up there. Joanne and her brother Junior had both told me they didn't want to interfere in Gerrick's affairs, but with him and their mother gone, what was holding them back?

I was dismayed and confounded, the news of my father's death starting to make its way through my body like a slow infection. Three days into it, I was crying inconsolably. It was as if my heart had been run over by a threshing machine. There wasn't a single bit that I could take comfort in. Lutrell held me as I cried. I clung to his steadfast devotion as if being airlifted from a wreck.

He asked if it would help if we could find out where my father had been buried and go to his gravesite, and I thought it might. I certainly wasn't eager to honor the man; it's that I felt as though I were freefalling and needed some tangible evidence of my father's existence in order to get my bearings. I had a father, a mother and a father; they were my progenitors. He was my parent whether he acted like it or not. Even if it were just a headstone, I needed a landing from which to get my bearings. Too much about my father had me flailing in the dark, wondering who he was and what had happened. The distress I felt was primal, instinctual, and ultimately just as formless as the man himself had been. I thought a grave would at least provide a concrete location where I could unload all my dead hopes.

To find my father's final resting place, I filed a request for a death certificate from the California Department of Vital Records; as his daughter with the court papers to prove it, I was entitled to a copy. When it arrived, I saw that he was buried near his home in the same cemetery as his wife, and that he had died of a heart attack in his home. But it also said that he had been diagnosed with metastatic lung cancer, so even if the heart attack was unexpected, he had to have known he was going to die soon. Apparently he had no desire to exit with a clear conscience in regard to his neglected children. He denied us until he was literally blue in the face.

The death certificate also stirred up some painful emotions relating to his money. It listed his occupation as "Investor," which jibed with several things I had been told. Some thirty years earlier, Margaret Pearl had said that my father wanted nothing to do with me because he was afraid I was after his money. And the private investigator I had hired right after publishing my novel mentioned that Gerrick Abbott had owned "a lot of property." At the time, I didn't want to hear about my father's finances because I didn't want my interest in meeting him to have anything to do with his bank accounts. Joanne at one point had remarked that her father wasn't a gambler but that he "played the stock market." Seeing "Investor" referenced on the death certificate confirmed my fear that money had played a role in why he rejected me. I was offended all over again that he may have kept me away because of some perceived moral failing on *my* part—projecting his own clutching greed onto me.

There were so many layers to how I felt about the man and our history. My grief again had me turning over every detail I could find to try and make sense of my father's absolute dereliction of duty. On the ancestry website where I learned of my father's death, there was only one picture of him, probably from around the time he was involved with my mother. He was good-looking: broad chested and square jawed, with a full head of sandy blond hair. He was standing next to three of his older brothers—my uncles—all of whom are now dead. In the picture, he looks as much like Sean as he did in that family portrait in Margaret Pearl's living room. But I can also see aspects of myself in him. There's a tilt to his head that causes him to look out of one eye more than the other, as if he's evaluating something. I can get that exact same expression. He's being a good sport, participating in the group photo, but his patience is wearing thin. Perhaps he wants the picture-taking business to be over with so he can get on to something more important. Whatever he's thinking about, it's not what's happening in that moment.

The person who created the family ancestry profile—a cousin—also created a genealogy tree, so I combed through it. The Abbott family tree identified seven siblings in my father's generation, not eight as Joanne had said. One of the children, in 1925, died on the day he was born. According to the genealogy dates, my paternal grandfather died when I was almost nine, and my grandmother died when I was sixteen, six months before my mother. I wonder if they knew about their son's affair with my mother. Did they know about Sean and me? What about all the aunts and uncles who were listed? Did none of them know? It's hard to believe that we weren't at least whispered about as family gossip. Was there ever any pushback, ever the slightest whiff of shame from any of them?

Again at the computer, I looked up the date when Gerrick married Margaret Pearl. I wanted to get the sequence of events straight in my head. A timeline emerged that continued to stink to high heaven. I learned that my father married Margaret Pearl on February 13, 1954. February 13 was also the anniversary day of my mother's divorce from Eugene Ellis. It was also the day, seared into my memory, when my mother drank with reckless abandon, had a heart attack, and was too intoxicated to do anything about it, thus dying in the car while sitting next to LG. My mother's father, the kindly looking man who divorced my maternal grandmother and then married her much older sister, had a February 14 birthday. LG's birthday was February 12. What a loaded couple of days that would have been for my mother—consciously or unconsciously.

I did the math. Apparently, nineteen-year-old Margaret Pearl was pregnant with Joanne two months before marrying twenty-two-year-old Gerrick Dean—what in those days would have been referred to as a shotgun wedding. Four years later, my mother had been divorced from her first husband, Eugene Ellis, when my father had her and his wife pregnant at the same time. Sean was born two months before Junior. A year after that, Margaret Pearl gave birth to her third child, and two months after *he* was born, I was conceived. Two months after I was born, my mother filed the paternity suit for child support, and won. What a mess. No wonder nobody was talking.

Next, to satisfy a perverse curiosity, I looked up my father's San Leandro home address, the one where I had met and talked to Mrs. Margaret Pearl Abbott. The house had been sold seven months after Gerrick's passing. I browsed through the photos in the real estate listing and saw that zero effort had been put into staging the property. Its decor was essentially unchanged from the 1980s when I'd first encountered it. There were the same old appliances, same dated wallpaper, tacky carpets, and musty-looking curtains. It did not look like the home of a wealthy man. In the family room where I had sat with Mrs. Abbott, imagining her as a stepmother of all things, all the furniture had been removed except for a large black flat-screen TV mounted to the wall and a pile of debris in the corner. When I looked closer I saw a wheelchair was in the pile. In the real estate photos! I couldn't believe that no one from the seller's agency had removed it, but in truth, it seemed kind of fitting. What a broken man. What a cripple he was, physically *and* emotionally. I was glad I saw the wheelchair and neglected home because it sealed my impression of so much blind dysfunction. Perhaps I was better off for never having gotten tangled up with such a family.

Still, it seemed odd that no effort had been made to sell the house for top dollar, considering all the hints that Gerrick Abbott was a wealthy man who had owned "a lot of property." I decided I really needed to get to the bottom of his finances. Was I right about his motives in keeping me away? And if so, just what kind of an inheritance was I missing out on?

I contacted the private investigator I had hired years earlier and asked him if he could elaborate on what he meant when he said that Gerrick had offloaded most of his property holdings before the real estate crash. After a couple of days, I received an electronic file that was basically a property-search-by-owner's name report. It was over half an inch thick and challenging to read; there were many Limited Liability Corporation names, various trust names and "Interfamily

Transfers." But from what I could tell, by the time my father died, he had sold between thirty and fifty *million* dollars' worth of unmortgaged property!

So the guy who had bailed out on paying my mother a measly ninety dollars a month in support for his two children had amassed a fortune by the end of his life. I couldn't look at his financial history any longer; it was all sickening and indefensible.

I've tried and tried, but I haven't been able to come up with a single excuse to make this go down easy. In the end, though, it really isn't about the money. True, I could do a lot with my fair share of fifty million dollars. But Lutrell and I are doing fine, and I've only known that Mr. Abbott was crazy rich for a few months, so obviously that hadn't been my main goal in seeking him out. And at the end of the day, no amount of money could make up for the fact that I'll never get the satisfaction of hearing Gerrick Abbott finally tell the truth to the people he had hurt.

So how was I going to make sense of all this? I had to find a way of putting to rest the incessant, now unanswerable, questions. If I didn't, I was afraid they would go on indefinitely, draining me, consuming me. I was still hoping that visiting my father's grave would provide some kind of closure, but I also felt like I needed something more, some public, and perhaps ceremonial, way to come to terms with the disappointing end of my journey. That's when another thought came to me: What if I had a funeral of sorts, not to eulogize Gerrick Dean Abbott Sr., but to finally step out of the shadows and declare publicly my right to have feelings about my missing father? I had to grieve not for the loss of the actual, mortal man, but for the loss of the relationship that might have been. Like burying a baby that was born dead, it would be a funeral for unrealized potential.

My pug-nosed naysayer held far less sway in my psyche than she once had, but she was still there with her finger wagging. How dare I have a funeral for someone I never knew and who had been dead for four years? Who in the world would ever come to such a dreadful occasion? It was terribly self-indulgent, wasn't it? I'd be laughed at, or even worse, pitied. The wet blanket of self-doubt was a garment I knew well, but I also knew that it was ultimately unproductive, and that I had thrown it off many other times before. Indeed, I wouldn't even *have* a life if I hadn't been able to do just that at many key junctures. So I started putting together a guest list for what I thought of as an alternative memorial ceremony of some kind.

As it happened, the news of my father's death came at the time of autumnal equinox, a time when the sun is level with the equator and the earth is equally divided between light and dark, night and day. I used that synchronicity to explain my reasons for coming together with friends while asking them to support me through my time of grief. The autumnal equinox is a time of balance, and balance was what I was after. I sent out invitations, and here is some of what I wrote in them:

Last month, I learned that my biological father died four years ago. Despite the various attempts I made to meet him, it never happened. All along, it was my hope that he would step out of the shadows and face his past—a past that included a long-term affair with my mother and the birth of my brother and me. For as long as I can remember, I have wanted my father to come forward not because he was forced but because he wanted to. Now, I must face the fact of his death and permanent silence. By acknowledging my grief in the company of friends, it is my intention to disavow the silence and shed light on the shadows.

In the spirit of moving on, and in observance of the autumnal equinox, a time when the sun shines directly on the equator, dividing day equally between light and dark, I am asking my friends to join me for a service of death and renewal, heart and healing, of reflection and appreciation. During this time of year, we celebrate the harvest and the abundance it brings. Fall is also a season of settling accounts, taking stock, and preparing for the days to come. It is a time of gratitude for blessings and a willingness to share that bounty with others.

As a part of this service, guests will have the opportunity to jot down a few words about any of their own past grievances or unresolved concerns on a piece of rice paper, and then we will drop the paper into water where it will melt, symbolically manifesting an intention of letting it go.

Following the service, there will be a potluck dinner in the adjacent Fellowship Hall.

As the "Yes, I will attend" RSVPs began to come in, I was encouraged. I invited Sean, but he wasn't interested. I could probably count on two hands the number of times he and I have visited together as adults; we just are not a part of each other's lives. He has his own path, and the funeral I was planning was not the place for us to bond. Deconstructing our story was my thing, not his.

A friend of mine is the minister of an enlightened local church that caters to the needs of the community with compassion and without dogma, and he agreed to officiate. At five o'clock on the designated Sunday evening, Lutrell, his father, stepmother, and aunt, along with several friends and I all gathered together in the sanctuary, a vaulted room with windows and skylights that had the amber hues of an autumn dusk streaming in.

My pastor/friend opened up by inviting each of us to reflect on our own experiences of grief and grievance, on unresolved and irresolvable dilemmas and wounds. He said that in times of sorrow we need to come together but rarely do so. We are expected to be strong, to tough it out, to make it quick, and get over it. "Well," he said, "that's not how grief works."

What I heard in his talk was how grievances don't heal with time or in isolation. What helps is having a community of people who are willing to love one another in times of tribulation as well as triumph. I took that as a sign to give up my stoic silence and pursue healthy connections where possible. Healing included being vulnerable and being seen. The minister also said something about how to achieve forgiveness that really cut to the heart of the matter for me. He said that forgiveness was "the willingness to give up all hope of a different outcome." Bingo. I had to forgive my riddle of a father and let go of my driving desire for a more satisfying conclusion to my search.

Then the pastor asked me to stand up and address those who had gathered for my benefit. *I can do this*, I told myself as I walked to the dais. After thanking everyone for coming, I explained how peculiar it was to own grief over a man who made it abundantly clear that he wanted nothing to do with me. But he wasn't just any man; he was my father. I told my friends that they were each invited to the service because I knew they were people I could trust. There had been so little honesty, virtue, or compassion in my forbearers, and my intention was, in the spirit of the equinox, to rebalance the scale. "I'm calling in the integrity forces on this one," I told the group, and there was an audible rustle of approval. They got me. We got each other. Even my friends who couldn't make it that day had assured me that they would be thinking about me, and I felt their love in the air. I was appealing to everyone's integrity not only for myself but also for my whole family, Abbott, Ellis, and G's included, past and present. "Help me heal the corrosive poisoning of silence," was my prayer.

Before anyone had arrived, I had prepared a tureen of water by infusing it with milk, honey, and lavender oil, a soft landing for the hard truths it was about to receive. The lavender oil had special meaning for me because it had been distilled by my father-in-law, Donald, at his ranch in the adjacent town of Napa. The water bath was for the letting-go ceremony that I had promised in my invitation. Before everybody assembled, I privately dunked one slip of water-soluble rice paper into the tureen. It had several names written on it, many of them Abbotts. Once the paper melted, I ladled a small amount of water into a tiny bottle to pour onto my father's grave, a final gesture of moving on from the idealized man and family members that never materialized.

During the service, my guests were given a few minutes to write whatever they wanted on their own slips of rice paper. Every single guest came forward with something.

Once we returned to our seats, the room settled in somber reflection. The pastor then asked if anyone wanted to share what they had written. I wasn't sure how audience participation was going to go over, but then my girlfriend's husband raised his hand and opened up. I would never have pegged him for being the sharing type, but he was so moved by the proceedings, he said. He explained how, when he was a child, his mother had died, and the pain at the time was so great that nobody ever talked about it. He agreed with the pastor that the passage of time had done little to banish his grief and said that it felt good to have an opportunity to reflect on his mother now.

A second person spoke up, truly shaken as she described forgiving herself for her fifty-year loveless marriage. Another talked about her self-imposed isolation and how grateful she was to be a part of the gathering. Yet another spoke about the pain of being rejected by parents for reasons she still didn't understand. Without exception, everyone, a mixture of folks who knew me but not each other, expressed appreciation for the supportive atmosphere and the opportunity to revisit, if not purge, unresolved issues in their lives.

Then my eighty-five-year-old father-in-law, who was sitting in the first pew, stood up and faced the group. Many of my friends knew that he had recently been suffering from dementia, so I don't think I was alone in wondering how this would go. He was capable of completely coherent moments, but he could also be quite distracted and forgetful at times. Even at his best, he was the picture of reserve and not one to freely express his emotions.

He's a big man, standing over six feet tall, and his movements were slow but dramatic and intentional. Watching him rise quickened my pulse. It almost felt like a father-of-the-bride moment. He introduced himself and, in his deep, resonant voice, made a small self-deprecating statement to put everyone at ease. "Forgive me if I wax philosophical . . . but that is what I do." Then he said that he just wanted to tell the group how much he appreciated me. He said it was unfortunate that my natural father had missed out on getting to know the wonderful daughter he had, and how grateful *he* was to have me as his daughter-in-law.

That heartfelt declaration was a spectacular conclusion to the service. I was filled to bursting with love and gratitude for him, for my husband and in-law family, and for all of my supportive friends. Their light was the counterpoint to my father's dark. For many years as I had worked my way through a maze of kinship dead ends and obstacles, I would lean on the phrase "We can pick our friends, but we can't pick our families." I was keenly aware that night of how stellar my friends are. We aren't bound by blood; we're bound by shared values, common interests, and above all, mutual respect. We each want the other to be happy, to be a success, to live life to the fullest. When a burden becomes heavy, we help each other carry the load. I hadn't gotten any of that from either my mother or father, and I'm pretty sure they never had friends who could provide that for them. That evening, I realized that I was the lucky one, and that I had found a balm for my pain in this wonderful supportive community.

Finally, it was time to eat, and what a glorious potluck feast it was. By the end of the day, I was deeply satisfied in both body and soul.

The next day, Lutrell and I hiked into some nearby woods with the lavender water filled with the group's reflections. I wanted to release it to Mother Nature's care. I recited one of the few prayers I've ever memorized, the Serenity Prayer: "God, grant me the serenity to accept the things I cannot change, the courage to change the things I can, and the wisdom to know the difference." It seemed fitting, given all I had learned over the decades of searching for answers. I had learned that I couldn't control my father, or anyone else, in any way, shape, or form. That was a fact, and I best make peace with it if I wanted to gain serenity. I also wanted to recognize the courage I had summoned to challenge and reject the bastard-daughter imprint I had been stamped with at birth. I had nothing to be ashamed of, and that prayer was a gentle reminder to hold onto the wisdom I had gained in knowing the difference.

We then drove to Hayward to find my father's final resting place. It was a trippy coincidence when I realized that it was the same cemetery where LG's parents had ended up: a massive complex of fifty or more manicured acres with sculpture gardens, numerous columbaria, a mausoleum, a crematorium, chapels, and offices. We went to the registration office, where I asked about both Mr. Abbott and LG's parents. A friendly young employee escorted us to each site. Along the way, he wanted to make small talk and, naturally, asked about my connection to the people I had come for. I didn't lie; I told him I was Mr. and Mrs. G's step-granddaughter and Abbott's daughter. It was the first time I laid claim to those facts without feeling defensive. About Abbott, I just said, "He was my father, but I never knew him." The clerk took my statement in stride without questioning me further, and I appreciated his discretion.

He unlocked the door into a cement monolith, the mausoleum where my father's remains had been entombed. The interior was a labyrinthine structure of granite-lined passageways; even our guide became turned around for a moment, shyly acknowledging his missteps. Arriving at the center of the structure, we found ourselves in front of a twenty-foot-high wall of marble-faced crypts, one of which was labeled "Abbott."

I saw my father's nameplate halfway up the polished stone surface. It was a combination marker for both him and his wife. She had predeceased him by five years, but their names were together on one placard—Abbott across the top, Margaret P. and Gerrick D. on the next line, and their birth and death years below that. The marker contained no epitaphs, nor even their middle names or their full birth or death dates. I had no way of knowing how that decision had been made, but it struck me as symbolic of who I had come to understand my father to be—withholding, to say the least.

Many of the other crypts and niches were adorned with personalized identifiers and mementos: hand-drawn pictures, cards, photographs; peel-and-stick hearts, stars, a yellow smiley face on one; a bunny, Easter eggs, and a cupcake on another. Some had loving messages written on them with felt-tipped markers. In contrast, the Abbott's square on the wall was sadly void except for an attached brass vase that held two artificial white roses.

There was no earthen grave to pour my grievance-laced lavender water. I also noticed that the only flowers inside the mausoleum were either silk or plastic. I had brought some real flowers with me but figured that real ones weren't allowed for some reason, so that was another gesture that would go unmade. I was trying to take it all in but struggled to connect with any real emotion. The only thoughts that surfaced seemed about as sterile as the place itself.

After a few minutes, a janitor lady approached and asked if I would like her to put the flowers I was clutching into the provided vase. "Could you?" I responded, grateful for her offer. She located an extension pole to get the vase down and chuckled when I told her that I wasn't sure if living flowers were even allowed. She then assured me that she would keep an eye on them. "Don't worry," she said with the utmost sincerity. "I won't let those go bad up there. I'll take care of them. Don't worry." It was obvious to me that she was the type of person and employee that did her job to the best of her ability. It didn't matter that the work was menial labor; she regarded her role of maintaining that pristine environment as a solemn duty, and she did it with pride. I liked her right away. We walked together over to a small utility closet where she had a sink, cleaning supplies, and wouldn't you know, pruning snips. She integrated my real flowers with the two fake roses as artfully as any trained florist.

After hanging the flowers next to the Abbotts' nameplate, the woman stood back to admire how nice they looked. "How do you know them?" she asked. When I told her he was my father, she was ever so slightly taken aback, as if perhaps she was afraid she hadn't been respectful enough of my sadness.

"But I never knew him," I was quick to add. I then said, "I bet you've heard all sorts of stories about the people in here."

"Oh, yes. We hear many stories. We have lots of different people; that's for sure."

She then went on to tell Lutrell and me about how, as an employee, she had been able to purchase one of the crypts for a very low price. "But you know," she said, "I told my daughter, I've been here for over forty years; I don't want to be here for the rest of eternity, so we sold it!" Her comedic timing was brilliant, and all three of us saw both the humor and seriousness of what she had said. She was the absolute opposite of that part of the Abbotts I had come to know, and her unguarded demeanor was manna from heaven. There was nothing I could do about the circumstances that had brought me to this moment, but I was willing to let the loving spirit of that woman, and whatever benevolent forces move time forward, heal us all: past, present, and future.

By the end of the day, I felt as though I had been belched from the belly of a beast. But I had one more task to fulfill. Before leaving the grounds, I poured my tiny bottle of lavender water next to a fountain outside the mausoleum. Part of the Lord's Prayer came to mind, "Forgive us our trespasses as we forgive those who trespass against us." It felt as right as it could. I haven't really forgiven my father, or any of the

Abbotts for that matter, but I'm willing to let a power greater than myself have a crack at it. I don't even know the whole Abbott vs. Ellis story, and I never will. All I know is that I'm ready to move on.

EPILOGUE

L ife sure does surprise us sometimes. I never had, and never will have, a father, but the past few years have brought me a lovely substitute that I didn't see coming.

My father-in-law, Donald Harms, was born in 1932, a year after Gerrick Dean Abbott. Coincidentally, Donald was also from Illinois. Like so many of his "silent generation," Donald tended to be undemonstrative, self-reliant, and hard to read. I used to tell my friends that he reminded me of the tight-lipped man holding a pitchfork in the *American Gothic* painting. And our relationship was just what you might expect: arid. Even though he and his wife (my husband's stepmother) live less than twenty miles from me and Lutrell, we only saw each other about four times a year: Donald's birthday, Lutrell's birthday, Father's Day, and Christmas or Thanksgiving.

On those occasions, Donald would allow me to hug him hello, but he would never hug back; he just stood there with his arms down, waiting for it to end. With his son, he would extend a formal handshake, but also no embrace. And at the dinner table, there would be little or no talking; the only noise came from silverware clinking against the plates. It wasn't that Donald was mean, or unhappy to see us; he just didn't have much to say. There was a time when I felt I needed to perk things up, so I'd become extra talkative. But I would always end up feeling foolish, like a court jester doing tricks. It was exhausting, and so I made the decision to stop doing it—and to stop caring if the room went silent.

But then, more than twenty years from when I first met Donald, there was an unexpected thaw in the ice. Donald had enjoyed a lifelong and successful career as an architect, and apparently, in addition to that, he had been ruminating for over fifty years on a certain chair form of his own mid-century modern design. He had a scaled drawing of it, but he had never quite been able to make it work. Once he retired though, the chair idea surfaced with enough urgency that he decided to bring it up with Lutrell, who by then had enjoyed a long career as a race car mechanic. I couldn't make heads or tails out of Donald's illustrations, but within twenty-four hours, Lutrell had crafted the first miniature prototype using tape and a wire hanger.

When Lutrell showed Donald what he had come up with, it was as if Donald saw his son for the very first time. He seemed surprised to discover just how accomplished Lutrell had become while he wasn't looking. Soon the two were spending hours together discussing engineering principles, the tensile strength of different metal options, art history, and furniture design. They eventually created a full-size prototype of the chair and applied, as business partners, for a design patent from the U.S. Patent Office. Five decades after the original inspiration, Donald and Lutrell, as collaborators, were granted ownership rights to the design.

This rapprochement between father and son was followed by an interesting turn in my own relationship with Donald. Donald was no longer a practicing architect, but he still owned and managed a commercial building in downtown Napa with twelve tenants. But around the time that he and Lutrell were working on the chair, Donald's secretary decided to retire.

Given my history of accounting and running my own hair salons, Donald asked if I could come in once a month to help him track the rents and balance the checkbooks. I was happy to. We agreed he would pay me for my time so that we could keep business and family separate.

Even though I only worked for Donald one day a month, I began having more one-on-one contact with him than I had in all my previous years of being married to his son. It didn't take long before I realized that Donald's dementia was starting to take a toll. He was not tracking details the way he once had. He'd mail the gas and electric payment in the phone company's envelope; he'd forget to record checks he was writing. If a person spoke too quickly on the answering machine, he couldn't grasp what they were saying. In order to stay on top of the routine dealings of the office, I bumped up to twice a month, then it was once a week, and at a turning point, when the inexorable creep of his aging was undeniable, I was going in twice a week. And all that regular contact led to a noticeable change in our relationship.

As his cognitive connective tissue was loosening and our interactions became more frequent, he came to depend on me more and more, and I lapped it up like cool water on a hot day. Donald is a proud gentleman who didn't want to be babied, so I stepped in only when he asked. But whenever I did augment his thoughts, or finish a sentence for him, or supply a missing word, he'd be visibly grateful and relieved.

He continued to decline, and the chaos that resulted in the office was putting more and more pressure on us all. It got to the point where I had to tell him I was going to quit at the end of the year. I said that I just didn't have the level of expertise to handle the workload. I was surprised by his reaction. He wanted to know who had undermined my confidence so that he could tell him or her to stop it. Nobody had; it was my decision, but I have to admit, I was thrilled to realize how much I had come to mean to the guy. Still, I knew I had to go, so he hired a management firm to run the building. But that didn't change things between us. In fact, over time, our relationship got even stronger.

More and more, when a situation came up that he couldn't remember how to handle, he'd look at me in all seriousness and ask, "What would *you* do?" I felt valued, and I couldn't get enough. The two of us were meeting at an interesting nexus in our lives, a time when his ego was relaxing and mine had strengthened. I'm in my fifties, and I no longer go around like a kid, asking if it's okay that I exist. I have confidence in my ability to speak my mind, and Donald appreciates that about me. And while it's not in his nature to draw *me* out, I know he's listening because of the way he leans in to catch every word. If he doesn't understand something, he always asks me to repeat it. He doesn't want to miss a single thing I say.

With his memory issues progressing, I suggested something to Donald that would eventually provide the ultimate emotional glue in our relationship. Donald had grown increasingly concerned about his own mortality, and he wanted to leave a record of his life for his children, stepchildren, grandson, step-grandsons, and great-grandchildren. I offered to start interviewing him about his life to create an autobiographical sketch, and aware that his memory was fading fast, he agreed to get started right away.

I adored the interviewing process. I could ask him anything, and I could tell he was getting a kick out of my curiosity. He told me about growing up on a farm in Illinois. He attended the same one-room schoolhouse for all seven of his elementary grades, and he had the same teacher the whole time, his beloved Mrs. Lockner. We discussed his architectural training in the early 1950s, the apex of the mid-century modern era. His instructors were like a who's who of the field: Mies van der Rohe, Charles Eames, Buckminster Fuller, George Matsumoto, Frank Lloyd Wright, Marcel Breuer, Eduardo Catalano, Horacio Caminos, and more. We got into his courtship with Lutrell's mother and the pain of their divorce in the 1960s. She left him, but he did what he could to maintain connections with his children as they were growing up.

Donald would circle around these same stories repeatedly, and it became my job to pluck the salient words and nuances from each version and compile them into a profile that captured the vibrancy of his life and character. He's a brilliant man, so even with diminished capacity there is still plenty of wit and insight in what he has to say. All of this from someone I had once thought of as cold and withholding! I got stories out of him that I knew even his wife hadn't heard, like when he told me about how his German grandmother enjoyed listening in on the telephone party line and would get upset when the people on the other end would start speaking *hochdeutsch*, or high German, instead of *plattdeutsch*, the German spoken in the low country where she was from. He told me about how, when he was a little boy, he once whacked his dog with a toy rake. He actually teared up from the guilt he still felt about it. And I got to hear about what it was like when the adults at church heard Pearl Harbor had been bombed, how he understood from their expressions that something terribly serious had happened.

One afternoon, we went out to lunch together, just the two of us, a first. I couldn't have been prouder sitting in that restaurant with this charming gent. We could hardly take bites of our food for all of the talking we were doing. The people around us were obviously curious who we were, because we appeared to be having too much fun to simply be father and daughter. He was no longer the pitchfork Donald of old, and I cherished every minute.

By the time I learned that my biological father had died, Donald and I were well and truly friends, and there was nothing I would hesitate to say to him. A couple of days after I got the news, I picked Donald up for work, and when he got in the car and asked how I was, I said that I had just received "funky news." I told him that it had me "pretty upset," as I fought back tears. I had to remind Donald that I had never met my father, and I was born of an extramarital affair. Donald showed polite regret for my loss but then said, "Terry, I don't mean to be cruel, but I have to tell you, back then, men just wanted to have sex." His frankness put a smile on my face. He wasn't being rude or cruel; he was sharing his honest, unfiltered opinion, and he trusted that I would take it as it was intended. I told him that I understood what he was saying, and I understood that without birth control, sex could get complicated very quickly back then. I then asked him if it made a difference to him that my mother had two children with this married man, and that the affair lasted at least three years. At that, Donald's tone did become graver when he said, "Oh. Yes, that is different." It was validating to have my father-in-law, a peer of my father's, acknowledge a difference between "boys being boys" and years of indiscretion. But he didn't want to leave me with that sadness, so he added, "It was the times, and men could be cads."

For so many years, I had wanted nothing more from my father than to be seen, acknowledged, and cared about. It never happened, yet here I was, getting those affirmations from this lovely and loving man, an individual who for years had been little more than a perfunctory relation. He now holds me so dear, and really, isn't that how a father is supposed to feel about his daughter? So I guess I finally got what I wanted, not when I thought I needed it the most but in all the ways that truly matter.

ACKNOWLEDGMENTS

Thinking about my life experiences, pulling them apart, considering each piece, recalling finer details has been a rewarding mental exercise in that it allowed me to know myself more fully, but writing about those same examinations for public consideration has been a feat I never would have accomplished if it hadn't been for the invaluable, professional guidance of my editor, Nan Wiener. It was a constant comfort to me that while I was focusing on the trees, Nan had both the trees and forest in sight. There were times during the writing process when I thought this memoir just couldn't be written; it was too complicated and it was too emotionally demanding, but Nan's consistent encouragement tipped my confidence into positive territory, and here we are. Knowing I had Nan on my side was like holding the hand of a loving protector on the first day of school; I still had to do the work, but I knew I'd be okay. Thank you, Nan, for taking my writing seriously and believing this story was worth telling. My gratitude is endless.

There's no way around it: writing takes time, solitary time, thousands of hours prowling around my own thoughts, recalling incidents, remembering who and what was there, what was said and how it made me feel. Huge portions of my day can be spent distracted, barely present for the people around me. Add to that the ludicrous amount of solo keyboarding hours spent pursuing perfect sentences. Furthermore, all of the various forms of public outreach to create an audience for my writing have consumed massive swaths of time. During all of this immersion, nobody was put on hold more than my husband; he is my best friend. From our first date, over twenty-seven years ago, Lutrell has demonstrated his unwavering commitment to me and to us. He is the one who waits for me—no matter what. He is why I know how it feels to be loved. With him, I'm cherished. Together, we won love's lottery.

Throughout this memoir, I refer to my friends in general terms, but that was to maintain a tight narrative arc. You guys know who you are, and you all mean the world to me. Thank you for making me feel seen and loved.

I also want to take this opportunity to thank my visionary publisher, Brooke Warner, and the team at She Writes Press for all they do to promote diverse voices through the written word.

ABOUT THE AUTHOR

photo credit: J. Sanborn Photography

Terry Sue Harms has been a hairdresser and salon owner for over forty years. After a childhood of illiteracy, she taught herself to read and write as a young adult, one of her proudest and most rewarding accomplishments. She has self-published two books: *Pearls My Mother Wore: A Novel* and *Reflections Upon the Occasion of My 85th Year*, a memoir coauthored with her father-in-law. Terry Sue lives in scenic Sonoma, California, with her husband. This is her third book.

SELECTED TITLES FROM SHE WRITES PRESS

She Writes Press is an independent publishing
company founded to serve women writers everywhere.
Visit us at www.shewritespress.com.

The Butterfly Groove: A Mother's Mystery, A Daughter's Journey by Jessica Barraco. $16.95, 978-1-63152-800-2. In an attempt to solve the mystery of her deceased mother's life, Jessica Barraco retraces the older woman's steps nearly forty years earlier—and finds herself along the way.

I'm the One Who Got Away: A Memoir by Andrea Jarrell. $16.95, 978-1-63152-260-4. When Andrea Jarrell was a girl, her mother often told her of their escape from Jarrell's dangerous, cunning father as if it was a bedtime story. Here, Jarrell reveals the complicated legacy she inherited from her mother—and shares a life-affirming story of having the courage to become both safe enough and vulnerable enough to love and be loved.

The Sportscaster's Daughter: A Memoir by Cindi Michael. $16.95, 978-1-63152-107-2. Despite being disowned by her father—sportscaster George Michael, said to be the man who inspired ESPN's *SportsCenter*—Cindi Michael manages financially and heals emotionally, ultimately finding confidence from within.

Veronica's Grave: A Daughter's Memoir by Barbara Bracht Donsky. $16.95, 978-1-63152-074-7. A loss and coming-of-age story that follows young Barbara Bracht as she struggles to comprehend the sudden disappearance and death of her mother and cope with a blue-collar father intent upon erasing her mother's memory.

Implosion: Memoir of an Architect's Daughter by Elizabeth W. Garber. $16.95, 978-1-63152-351-9. When Elizabeth Garber, her architect father, and the rest of their family move into Woodie's modern masterpiece, a glass house, in 1966, they have no idea that over the next few years their family's life will be shattered—both by Woodie's madness and the turbulent 1970s.